THE DHARMIC ECONOMY

A New Paradigm for Inclusive Growth

Dr.Prasanta Mujrai

Copyright © 2024 Dr.Prasanta Mujrai

All rights reserved

The characters and events portrayed in this book are fictitious. Any similarity to real persons, living or dead, is coincidental and not intended by the author.

No part of this book may be reproduced, or stored in a retrieval system, or transmitted in any form or by any means, electronic, mechanical, photocopying, recording, or otherwise, without express written permission of the publisher.

ISBN-13: 9798302762566

Introduction

"The Dharmic Economy: A New Paradigm for Inclusive Growth" is a groundbreaking exploration of how ancient wisdom can shape the future of global economic systems. In this thought-provoking book, the author presents a compelling case for integrating the timeless principles of Dharma—justice, ethical responsibility, and holistic well-being—into modern economic frameworks. Drawing from the rich traditions of Eastern philosophy, this book offers an innovative approach to fostering sustainable and inclusive growth, where prosperity is not measured merely by material wealth, but by the flourishing of all people and the planet. With a perfect blend of spirituality and pragmatism, *The Dharmic Economy* challenges conventional thinking and inspires a new vision for a more equitable, compassionate, and harmonious global economy. This book is a must-read for anyone seeking to transform the way we think about growth, progress, and the true meaning of prosperity.

The Dharmic Economy: A New Paradigm for Inclusive Growth
By
Dr.Prasanta Mujrai

Contents
Chapter 1: Understanding Dharma in the Modern Context
Chapter 2: The Limitations of Current Economic Models
Chapter 3: Principles of the Dharmic Economy
Chapter 4: The Four Purusharthas and Economic Life

Chapter 5: Karma Economics: Action and Consequence
Chapter 6: Ethical Leadership in the Dharmic Economy
Chapter 7: Conscious Capitalism: A Dharmic Approach
Chapter 8: Sustainable Business Practices
Chapter 9: Fair Trade and Ethical Supply Chains
Chapter 10: Mindful Marketing and Advertising
Chapter 11: Ethical Banking and Finance
Chapter 12: Socially Responsible Investing
Chapter 13: Alternative Currencies and Local Economies
Chapter 14: Philanthropy and Dana (Giving)
Chapter 15: Wealth Distribution and Economic Equality
Chapter 16: The Concept of Swadharma in Career Choices
Chapter 18: Fair Labor Practices and Workers' Rights
Chapter 19: Education and Skill Development
Chapter 20: Artificial Intelligence and the Future of Work
Chapter 21: Dharmic Governance Models
Chapter 22: Economic Policy Through a Dharmic Lens

Chapter 23: Global Cooperation and Trade
Chapter 24: Taxation and Public Finance
Chapter 25: Legal Frameworks for the Dharmic Economy
Chapter 26: Technology and Innovation in the Dharmic Economy
Chapter 27: Urban Planning and Sustainable Communities
Chapter 28: The Dharmic Economy in a Post-Scarcity World
Chapter 29: Global Challenges and Dharmic Solutions
Chapter 30: Personal Transformation for a Dharmic Economy

Chapter 1: Understanding Dharma in the Modern Context

Defining dharma and its relevance today

Dharma has been an important and complex idea in religion and philosophy for thousands of years. The term's intricate and subtle implications in Sanskrit make it difficult to translate into English or other European languages. Integral to Dharmaaviors and deeds are concepts like duty, virtue, ethics, and leading a virtuous life; they encompass all that is in line with the cosmic order.

Dharma, the religious and moral code that regulates one's actions, is one of the four main aims of human existence in Hinduism, which is known as purushartha. Truthfulness and nonviolence are examples of universal principles (sadharana dharma) that everyone must adhere to. Each person also has special obligations (svadharma) that are related to their societal function, life stage, and personal circumstances. This multi-faceted view of dharma offers a thorough basis for developing one's character and making ethical decisions.

Beyond Hinduism, other Indian faiths like Jainism and Buddhism also place a strong emphasis on the notion of dharma. One of the Three Jewels (Triratna) that Buddhists look to for guidance is dharma, which refers to the teachings and universal truths declared by the Buddha. In addition to its more conventional definition as moral goodness, dharma has a distinct connotation in Jainism as an everlasting essence that permits entities to move.

Because it offers a comprehensive framework for ethics, social responsibility, and sustainable living, dharma has the ability to solve modern problems. Applying the principles of dharma can help contemporary society find a way to overcome challenges like economic injustice, moral ambiguity, and environmental damage.

The centrality of dharma's teachings on responsibility and

obligation is one reason for its continued relevance in modern times. The dharmic worldview calls attention to people's responsibilities to one another, to the environment, and to the universe at large in a time when people are more likely to act in their own self-interest. An approach to solving global problems that is more sustainable and interdependent can be fostered by taking a larger perspective of human responsibility.

In addition, dharma offers a framework for making ethical decisions that transcends simple moral absolutes and inflexible norms. The opposite is true: it exhorts people to become wise and prudent, to consider all angles of a problem and behave in a way that promotes harmony and balance. When faced with the complicated moral challenges of today, a sophisticated approach to ethics is vital.

Sustainable lifestyles and caring for the environment are two areas where the notion of dharma may provide light. In line with modern environmental ethics, the ancient Indian view of people as guardians, not owners, of the natural world might guide us toward more sustainable methods of managing our resources and advancing our economy.

Dharmic principles can offer a balance to economic and political systems that are dominated by materialistic or self-serving ideologies. For example, dharmic capitalism advocates for economic policies that help people reach their full potential while simultaneously tackling problems of inequality and social welfare, with a focus on the ethical production and distribution of wealth.

at addition, at a time when so much emphasis is placed on outward accomplishments and monetary success, the dharmic focus on inward development and self-realization provides a refreshing viewpoint. Dharma offers a way to personal development and fulfillment that goes beyond monetary wealth by urging people to develop virtues like knowledge, bravery, and compassion.

The evolution of dharmic principles in economic thought

A intriguing junction of ancient knowledge and current concerns is the growth of dharmic ideas in economic theory. This development is traceable from the first Vedic writings all the way up to modern understandings of dharmic economics via classical literature such as Kautilya's Arthashastra.

Among the four great aspirations of ancient Indian philosophy were artha, or worldly riches and success, dharma, or righteousness, kama, or pleasure, and moksha, or release. This all-encompassing perspective recognized the significance of financial security within a larger moral and spiritual context.

One of the oldest and most thorough treatises on statecraft and economics in the Indian tradition is Kautilya's Arthashastra, which was composed about the 2nd century BCE. There are significant similarities between this text and current economic theory in its extensive tenets of government, taxes, and economic management. For example, a notion that is still important to contemporary finance theory—the link between risk and interest rates—was addressed by Kautilya.

Budgetary restraint was another theme running through the Arthashastra, which cautioned that government spending shouldn't go beyond a specific percentage of GDP. Even in modern debates over public finance, this early understanding of the importance of balanced budgets and effective leadership is crucial.

An emphasis on a middle ground between monetary success and ethical concerns has persisted throughout the development of Indian economic thinking. One solution that has evolved to the problem of how to balance economic development with social responsibility is the idea of dharmic capitalism, which places an emphasis on the ethical production and distribution of wealth. This method aims to find a middle ground between two extremes—total state control and unrestrained capitalism—by highlighting the importance of markets while simultaneously tackling problems of sustainability and equality.

Modern times have called for a reinterpretation of dharmic economic ideas to meet the problems of today. For instance, contemporary ideas of sustainable resource management are in line with the traditional Indian perspective that land (called Vasudha or Vasundhara) is a source of wealth rather than money itself. This view promotes a more comprehensive and long-term strategy for economic growth, one that takes into account social and environmental repercussions in addition to financial gains. There are similarities between contemporary economic theory and the dharmic emphasis on cyclicality, which is expressed in the idea of karma. Modern methods of macroeconomic management are consistent with the observation of economic cycles and the requirement for adaptable governmental responses depending on the phase of the cycle in question.

Also, dharmic economics promotes looking at human motivation and happiness from several angles. It admits that selfishness plays a part, but it also acknowledges that other motivators, including duty, compassion, and the pursuit of spiritual enlightenment, play a larger role. With this complex view of people, we may craft economic policies that take into account people's material, social, and psychological demands.

The idea of incorporating dharmic ideas into contemporary economic systems has gained popularity in recent years. There has been a movement towards more comprehensive evaluations of social welfare, motivated by dharmic principles, and ideas like "gross national happiness" and "beyond GDP" are examples of this trend.

An additional theme running through the development of dharmic economic theory is the significance of moral reasoning and personal character when it comes to making financial decisions. If we want to build a community that is really successful and peaceful, we must cultivate qualities like self-control, generosity, and compassion. In addition to policy-driven or structural reforms, this emphasis on personal development as a basis for economic prosperity is a great asset.

Bridging ancient wisdom with contemporary challenges
Finding common ground between traditional dharmic knowledge and modern problems calls for careful consideration of all angles. To do this, one must first determine which dharma principles are universally applicable and then modify or reinterpret these principles in light of the specific challenges posed by the contemporary world.
The field of environmental stewardship is an important one where dharmic knowledge may guide modern practice. There is a strong congruence between contemporary ecological ethics and the ancient Indian concept of people being guardians, not proprietors, of the natural world. A change from short-term exploitation to conservation and regeneration may be encouraged by adopting this viewpoint, which can assist develop more sustainable approaches to resource management.
Some of the problems with economic systems that are either overly dependent on market forces or overly regulated by the state can be alleviated by applying dharmic principles. For example, dharmic capitalism provides a compromise that allows for the importance of markets and personal initiative without sacrificing ethics or social duty. Policies that foster economic growth while simultaneously tackling inequality and environmental sustainability can be informed by this approach.
An important balance to radical individualism is the dharmic stress on responsibility and obligation. At a time when we must all work together to solve global problems, the dharmic view urges people to think about what they owe to the world around them. A stronger feeling of global citizenship and collective accountability to combat climate change and social inequity can emerge from this.
The fields of leadership and governance are another area where traditional knowledge may shed light on contemporary methods. Public and commercial sector leaders can learn from the dharmic ideal of the just ruler, who acts in accordance with

universally accepted standards of fairness and care for the well-being of everyone. Corruption and self-interest among those in authoritative positions can be mitigated in this way.

When faced with the many moral challenges of today's society, the dharmic method of ethics—which places an emphasis on wisdom and judgment instead of strict regulations—is especially helpful. In domains like business, healthcare, and technology, this nuanced approach may guide the development of increasingly complex frameworks for making ethical decisions.

When it comes to self-improvement, dharmic principles provide helpful guidance for making it through the hectic, demanding modern world without sacrificing harmony or fulfillment. A counterpoint to the materialistic emphasis of much modern society is the emphasis on inward development, mindfulness, and the cultivation of virtues.

Another domain where dharmic knowledge may make a big splash is education. More all-encompassing educational methods that equip students for lifelong learning might be informed by the holistic approach to learning embraced by ancient Indian traditions. This approach prioritizes character development alongside intellectual advancement.

More successful methods to peacebuilding and reconciliation can be informed by the dharmic ideals of nonviolence, compassion, and connectivity in the field of conflict resolution. When applied to a society where ideological and cultural differences are common, these ideas can pave the way for more conversation and mutual understanding.

Concepts like karma and the yuga cycles represent the dharmic knowledge of the cyclical nature of occurrences, which can guide more systemic and long-term ways of dealing with social and environmental problems. Instead than focusing on immediate benefits, this viewpoint stresses the need of thinking about how decisions will play out in the future.

When applied to the scientific and technical spheres, dharmic concepts can assist direct development in a way that prioritizes the well-being of all living things. New technologies, including genetic engineering and artificial intelligence, can be better handled with this information in hand.

Lastly, contemporary scientific insights in ecology and quantum physics are in harmony with the dharmic focus on the interdependence of all entities and occurrences. By looking at social and environmental problems through this lens, we may better understand the interconnected web of causes and effects and develop solutions that take this whole picture into account.

Finally, dharma provides a complex and comprehensive framework for dealing with modern problems. We can create more comprehensive, moral, and long-term strategies for individual growth, societal structure, and international crisis resolution if we combine traditional knowledge with contemporary scientific understanding. A vital resource for managing the complexity of the modern world, the continual evolution of dharmic thinking proves its enduring relevance and flexibility.

References:

1. Dharma. (n.d.). In Wikipedia. Retrieved November 30, 2024, from https://en.wikipedia.org/wiki/Dharma

2. Britannica. (n.d.). Dharma | Hinduism, Buddhism, Karma. Retrieved November 30, 2024, from https://www.britannica.com/topic/dharma-religious-concept

3. Balasubramanian, S. (2022). Kautilyanomics for Modern Times. The Institute of Secretariat Training and Management (ISTM). https://www.istm.gov.in/library/kautilyanomics

4. The Policy Circle. (n.d.). Indian economic thought: A less-understood and misunderstood legacy. Retrieved November 30, 2024, from https://www.policycircle.org/opinion/indian-economic-thought-legacy/

5. Swarajya. (n.d.). Hindunomics: From State To Wealth To Dharma To Happiness. Retrieved November 30, 2024, from https://swarajyamag.com/magazine/hindunomics-from-state-to-wealth-to-dharma-to-happiness

6. Benefiel, Z. (n.d.).

Bridging Ancient Wisdom and Modern Innovation for a Sustainable Future. Thinkers360. Retrieved November 30, 2024, from https://www.thinkers360.com/tl/blog/members/bridging-ancient-wisdom-and-modern-innovation-for-a-sustainable-future

7. Philosophy Talk. (n.d.). Ancient Wisdom for Modern Times. Retrieved November 30, 2024, from https://www.philosophytalk.org/shows/ancient-wisdom-modern-times

Chapter 2: The Limitations of Current Economic Models

Two main schools of thought in modern economic history —neoliberal capitalism and socialist economic models— have ruled the world stage. Both systems have flaws and limits, but they have also tried to solve social problems and boost the economy. This chapter delves into the criticisms leveled against neoliberal capitalism, socialist economies, and their respective flaws. It concludes by arguing that a compromise that takes the best parts of both systems and makes them better is necessary.

Critiquing Neoliberal Capitalism
Free markets, deregulation, privatization, and little government involvement are central tenets of neoliberal capitalism, the prevailing economic philosophy of the late 20th century. There is a lot of agreement that this paradigm has boosted innovation and economic progress, but there is also a lot of agreement that it has had harmful effects on society and the environment.

The idea that neoliberalism makes income disparity worse is one of the main arguments against it. The bulk of the population has seen their salaries remain stagnant and their economic chances decline as a result of neoliberal policies, according to Stiglitz (2019). This widening gap threatens both short- and long-term economic development and social stability, which in turn creates ethical questions.

More financial instability has been linked to the deregulation of financial markets, which is a fundamental principle of neoliberalism. "Capital deregulation has led to an increase in financial instability including economic events that, at times, have sent shockwaves around the world," an Investopedia article notes. The possible repercussions of unregulated financial liberalization are vividly shown by the 2008 global financial crisis.

The environmental impact of neoliberal policies has also been a point of criticism. The confidence in market solutions to environmental problems and the focus on short-term profit maximization have frequently resulted in the disregard of long-term ecological viability. In the words of Di Duca, "neoliberalism has commodified the planet's resources and led to companies producing at capacities that far outstretch the earth's limits".

Those who hold the view that neoliberalism's emphasis on markets and individuality weakens community ties and collective accountability have valid points. "Neoliberalism has frayed our collective bonds as it celebrates competitive self-interest and hyper-individualism, stigmatizes compassion and solidarity," says Lukacs, who is quoted in Di Duca's piece. Social cohesiveness and the capacity to tackle common problems may be severely impacted by this change in cultural norms.

Some people think that public services like healthcare and education have become commodities because of neoliberalism. since a result, issues of access and equity have been brought to light, since vital services are being subjected to market pressures instead of being recognized as basic rights.

In addition, neoliberal policies that promote free trade and globalization have been associated with the exploitation of developing-world workers and the loss of jobs in industrialized countries. Some say it improves the economy as a whole, while others worry about the impact on people's lives and how it will affect their communities.

According to studies conducted by Goudarzi et al. (2022), the general public's perspective on income inequality has evolved over time, with the help of neoliberal policies and institutions. Beyond the short-term effects on the economy, this discovery makes one wonder what kind of social consequences neoliberal philosophy can have in the long run.

The Shortcomings of Socialist Economies

Socialism as an economic system has its flaws, but it was once a viable alternative to capitalism that promised more social justice and equality. A number of serious drawbacks of centrally planned economies have been exposed by the many socialist experiments that took place throughout the twentieth century.

Ludwig von Mises initially stated the economic calculation issue, which is one of the most basic criticisms of socialist systems. For Mises, "a socialist system based upon a planned economy would not be able to allocate resources effectively due to the lack of price signals," as stated in the Britannica article. Central planners confront tremendous difficulties in effectively distributing resources and meeting consumer wants in the absence of a market system for pricing.

Efficiency and creativity have always been problems for socialist economies. Suppressing competition, as Milton Friedman said, is one way in which state control of the means of production may hinder technological advancement. Reduced productivity and slower economic growth can result from the bureaucratic character of centrally planned economies and the absence of market incentives.

Suppressing economic democracy and self-management is another major flaw of socialist economies. Even if central planning could solve its incentive and innovation difficulties, it would still fail miserably at maximizing economic democracy and self-management, as pointed out by Robin Hahnel. Workers' agency and group decision-making are central to socialist ideology, yet this restriction undermines both.

One argument against socialist systems is that they do nothing to encourage people to work hard and come up with new ideas. In the words of Mill, "in any society where everyone holds equal wealth, there can be no material incentive to work because one does not receive rewards for a work well done" . Less overall productivity and economic stagnation might result from this failure to differentiate.

There has been a lot of political authoritarianism throughout the history of socialist economies. Many tyrannical governments have come to power as a result of economic centralization, which has stifled individual liberties. The socialist principles of social fairness and equality are severely contradicted by this result.

There have been shortages and inefficiencies in socialist economies' production and distribution of commodities and services as well. Mismatches between supply and demand, caused by a lack of market signals, can cause undesirable items to be in abundance and desirable ones to be in low supply.

Centrally planned economies are also less equipped to adjust to new technology and shifting economic circumstances because of their inherent rigidity. A country's economic progress and global competitiveness might be stunted by this rigidity.

The Need for a Middle Path

More and more people are realizing that market processes have their limitations, and that social safeguards and community aims are better served by a socialist economy that strikes a balance between the two extremes. This method, which aims to combine the best features of both "market socialism" and "progressive capitalism," tries to fix the problems that both ideologies have.

"Progressive capitalism," the economic model put out by Joseph Stiglitz (2019), seeks to reestablish harmony among private enterprise, public administration, and civic engagement. This perspective acknowledges that markets may help people work together, but it stresses the significance of democratic oversight to stop exploitation and rent-seeking.

Private entrepreneurship and state investment are both acknowledged as important components of this medium route. The government, according to Stiglitz, should put money into fields like public health, education, and fundamental research since private companies either don't want to or can't. This well-rounded strategy can promote innovation and economic development while guaranteeing the proper provision of necessary public goods.

According to David Lane, market socialism provides a workable political path for a return to public ownership, mutualization, and suggestive planning over time. This strategy maintains a lot of the efficiency gains from market processes while increasing government oversight in important economic areas.

The necessity to combat income disparity and guarantee a fairer distribution of economic benefits is another tenet of the middle route. Some ways to achieve this goal include more equitable taxes, more robust social safety nets, and measures to provide educational and economic possibilities for all citizens.

An additional essential component of a well-rounded economic model is environmental sustainability. The environmental problems caused by neoliberal capitalism and conventional socialist models can be solved by finding a middle ground that promotes sustainable practices and includes the real costs of environmental deterioration in economic decision-making.

A middle ground between capitalism and socialist principles might be the idea of economic democracy, which calls for more worker input into ownership and decision-making processes. Efficient and equitable economic organization can be achieved using this method.

Additionally, a well-rounded economic model would put the welfare of society as a whole ahead of the maximizing of profits in the near term. By changing our attention away from the inflexible inefficiencies of centrally planned economies, we may alleviate some of the social and environmental problems that have worsened under neoliberal rule.

Targeted laws, public-private partnerships, and creative ownership structures like cooperatives and employee-owned firms would likely be part of the policy toolbox for a middle route approach's implementation. Because of its adaptability, it may be used in different economic situations and overcome different obstacles.

References

1. Britannica. (n.d.). Economic system – Problems with socialism. Retrieved November 30, 2024,

from https://www.britannica.com/money/economic-system/Problems-with-socialism

2. Di Duca, M. (n.d.). How Neoliberalism Destroyed the Planet and Why Capitalism Won't Save Us. Global Social Challenges. Retrieved November 30, 2024, from https://sites.manchester.ac.uk/global-social-challenges/2021/05/04/how-neoliberalism-destroyed-the-planet-and-why-capitalism-wont-save-us/

3. Goudarzi, S., Knowles, E. D., & Badaan, V. (2022). Neoliberal policies, institutions have prompted preference for greater income inequality. NYU. Retrieved November 30, 2024, from https://www.nyu.edu/about/news-publications/news/2022/may/neoliberal-policies--institutions-have-prompted-preference-for-g.html

4. Investopedia. (n.d.). Neoliberalism: What It Is, With Examples and Pros and Cons. Retrieved November 30, 2024, from https://www.investopedia.com/terms/n/neoliberalism.asp

5. Lane, D. (n.d.). Why market socialism is a viable alternative to neoliberalism. LSE Politics and Policy. Retrieved November 30, 2024, from https://blogs.lse.ac.uk/politicsandpolicy/37396/

6. Stiglitz, J. E. (2019, May 30). After Neoliberalism. Project Syndicate. Retrieved November 30, 2024, from https://www.project-syndicate.org/commentary/after-neoliberalism-progressive-capitalism-by-joseph-e-stiglitz-2019-05

7. Wikipedia. (n.d.). Criticism of socialism. Retrieved November 30, 2024, from https://en.wikipedia.org/wiki/Criticism_of_socialism

Chapter 3: Principles of the Dharmic Economy

A Dharmic economy is one that takes into account all aspects of society, including morality, religion, and economics. This approach presents an attractive substitute for socialism and neoliberal economic systems, drawing on the timeless teachings of Buddhist economics and Sanatana Dharma. The Dharmic economy is discussed in this chapter along three main points: the importance of interdependence and connection, the creation and distribution of wealth in an ethical manner, and the need to strike a balance between material advancement and spiritual growth.

Interconnectedness and Mutual Dependence

A fundamental tenet of Dharmic economic theory is the idea of interdependence and interconnection, which has its origins in the Buddhist non-substantiality perspective and the Sanatana Dharma's Atman and Brahman concepts. From this vantage point, it's clear that everything is interconnected and that no one thing can be considered independent.

When it comes to Buddhist economics, the non-substantial perspective shapes economic systems in deep ways. Avoiding the economic offenses, disputes, and deprivations that might result from limiting individualism, it promotes egoless-ness. It advocates, on the other hand, a mutually beneficial approach that acknowledges the interconnectedness of all economic players.

The Sanatana Dharma tenets of the unity of all beings—the atman, or soul, and brahman, or ultimate consciousness—are consistent with this outlook. A sense of harmony, compassion, and oneness with the cosmos is fostered by the understanding that Atman and Brahman are interdependent. This amounts to an acknowledgment, from an economic perspective, that people's activities in the market can have effects that extend much beyond their own short-term interests.

The supposed rational, self-interested economic actor in neoclassical economics, homo economicus, is called into question by the concept of interconnection. It argues instead that economic decisions should think about how they will affect more than just the economy. Stakeholder theory argues that companies should stop looking out for their shareholders' best interests and start prioritizing those of their workers, consumers, and suppliers as well as the community at large.

In practice, this principle can manifest in various ways:

1. Collaborative consumption and sharing economy models that maximize resource utilization and foster community bonds.
2. Circular economy approaches that minimize waste and environmental impact by designing products for reuse and recycling.
3. Fair trade practices that recognize the interdependence of producers and consumers across global supply chains.
4. Local economic development initiatives that strengthen community ties and resilience.

The Dharmic view of interconnectedness also extends to the relationship between the economy and the natural environment. It recognizes that economic activities are embedded within and dependent upon ecological systems. This perspective aligns with modern concepts of sustainable development and ecological economics, emphasizing the need for economic models that operate within planetary boundaries.

Ethical Wealth Creation and Distribution

By viewing wealth as a tool to carry out one's obligations to oneself, to society, and to the divine, the Dharmic perspective on wealth generation and distribution is ethically based. Artha, one of Sanatana Dharma's four Purusharthas, or life objectives, encapsulates this outlook.

In the Dharmic economy, the ethical development of wealth is governed by the principle of 'Karma,' which highlights the law of cause and effect. According to this notion, people should be held financially accountable for the results of their own acts. The belief is that 'Adharma,' or unrighteous, wealth gained via immoral activities like lying, stealing, or being dishonest leads to bad Karma.

An ancient legal document, the Manusmriti lays out principles for right and wrong behavior in the acquisition and distribution of money, among other areas of economic life. Recognizing that money acquired by dishonesty or exploitation has detrimental effects on both people and society, it stresses the significance of honesty, integrity, and justice in monetary interactions.

Key principles of ethical wealth creation in the Dharmic economy include:

1. Honest and fair business practices that prioritize value creation over mere profit extraction.

2. Sustainable resource utilization that considers long-term environmental and social impacts.

3. Innovation and entrepreneurship directed towards solving societal problems and enhancing collective well-being.

4. Fair compensation and treatment of workers, recognizing their dignity and contribution to wealth creation.

Regarding wealth distribution, the Dharmic economy emphasizes the concept of 'Dhana' or charity. Individuals are encouraged to share their wealth with those in need and contribute to the welfare of society through acts of philanthropy and generosity. This is not viewed merely as an act of benevolence but as a sacred duty and a means of accruing spiritual merit.

The Rigveda, one of the oldest scriptures of Sanatana Dharma, underscores the interconnectedness of wealth and societal well-being, suggesting that prosperity should be shared equitably to benefit all members of society. This aligns with modern concepts of inclusive growth and shared prosperity.

Practical applications of ethical wealth distribution in a

Dharmic economy might include:

1. Progressive taxation systems that ensure those who benefit most from society's infrastructure contribute proportionately.
2. Corporate social responsibility initiatives that go beyond tokenism to create meaningful social impact.

3. Employee ownership models and profit-sharing schemes that distribute the fruits of collective labor more equitably.

4. Social entrepreneurship and impact investing that direct capital towards addressing pressing societal challenges.

5. Universal basic services or income schemes that ensure a minimum standard of living for all members of society.

The Dharmic approach to wealth creation and distribution seeks to strike a balance between individual initiative and social responsibility, recognizing that true prosperity can only be achieved when it is shared broadly across society.

Balancing Material Progress with Spiritual Growth

The Dharmic economy stands out because of its unique focus on achieving a balance between worldly success and spiritual development. While monetary success is essential, this theory holds that it should not be seen as an aim in itself but as a means to an end—in this case, the attainment of spiritual enlightenment.

The four Purusharthas, or aims of human existence, in Sanatana Dharma are Kama (desires), Moksha (liberation), Artha (prosperity), and Dharma (righteousness). With its emphasis on the interconnectedness of one's physical, mental, and spiritual selves, this paradigm promotes a balanced way of living.

In a similar vein, the Buddhist economic paradigm stresses moderation and promotes a medium ground between extremes like austerity and consumerism. In support of a cooperative economy, it advocates meeting needs rather than satisfying greed.

Key aspects of balancing material progress with spiritual growth in a Dharmic economy include:

1. Redefining Progress: The Dharmic economy challenges narrow definitions of progress based solely on GDP growth. Instead, it advocates for broader measures of societal well-being that include indicators of environmental health, social cohesion, and spiritual fulfillment. This aligns with modern concepts like Gross National Happiness and the Beyond GDP movement.

2. Mindful Consumption: Encouraging consumption patterns that satisfy genuine needs rather than artificially created wants. This involves promoting mindfulness and contentment, countering the consumerist tendencies of modern market economies.

3. Work-Life Balance: Recognizing the importance of leisure, family time, and spiritual practices alongside productive work. This might involve policies promoting shorter working hours, sabbaticals for spiritual pursuits, or incorporating meditation and mindfulness practices in the workplace.

4. Education for Holistic Development: Integrating spiritual and ethical teachings into educational curricula alongside technical and professional skills. This aims to produce not just skilled workers but well-rounded individuals capable of contributing positively to society.

5. Ethical Business Practices: Encouraging businesses to adopt practices that not only generate profits but also contribute to the spiritual and ethical growth of employees and society at large. This might involve corporate policies that encourage volunteering, ethical decision-making, and spiritual practices.

6. Environmental Stewardship: Recognizing the spiritual dimension of humanity's relationship with nature and promoting economic practices that nurture and regenerate the natural environment.

The principle of balancing material progress with spiritual growth challenges the materialistic orientation of mainstream economic models. It suggests that true prosperity and well-being cannot be achieved through material accumulation alone but require a harmonious development of both material and spiritual aspects of life.

The principles of interconnectedness and mutual dependence, ethical wealth creation and distribution, and balancing material progress with spiritual growth form the foundation of a Dharmic economy. This approach offers a holistic alternative to current economic models, addressing many of their shortcomings while promoting a more sustainable, equitable, and fulfilling way of organizing economic life.

By recognizing the interdependence of all economic actors and their embeddedness in social and ecological systems, the Dharmic economy promotes a more collaborative and sustainable approach to economic development. Its emphasis on ethical wealth creation and distribution addresses issues of inequality and exploitation that plague many current economic systems. Finally, by balancing material progress with spiritual growth, it offers a more comprehensive vision of human well-being and societal progress.

As we grapple with the complex challenges of the 21st century, including climate change, inequality, and social fragmentation, the principles of the Dharmic economy offer valuable insights for reimagining our economic systems. While implementing these principles on a large scale would require significant shifts in policy, business practices, and individual behavior, they provide a compelling vision for a more balanced, ethical, and sustainable economic future.

References

1. Artfactory. (2024, November 21). Unveiling the Core Principles of Sanatan Dharma: Timeless Truths for a Balanced Life. Artfactory Blog. https://artfactory.in/blog/

core-principles-of-sanatan-dharma
2. Adikka Channels. (n.d.). Ethical Principles Of Wealth Management In Sanatana Dharma. https://adikkachannels.com/ethical-principles-of-wealth-management-in-sanatana-dharma/
3. India Foundation. (n.d.). Buddhist Economics of Compassion and Communion. https://indiafoundation.in/articles-and-commentaries/buddhist-economics-of-compassion-and-communion/
4. Swarajya. (n.d.). Hindunomics: From State To Wealth To Dharma To Happiness. https://swarajyamag.com/magazine/hindunomics-from-state-to-wealth-to-dharma-to-happiness
5. The Gaudiya Treasures of Bengal. (2023, March 16). What is Dharma? The Key to Finding Balance, Happiness and Purpose in Life. https://thegaudiyatreasuresofbengal.com/2023/03/16/what-is-dharma-the-key-to-finding-balance-happiness-and-purpose-in-life/

Chapter 4: The Four Purusharthas and Economic Life

The concept of the four Purusharthas - Dharma (righteousness), Artha (wealth), Kama (desire), and Moksha (liberation) - provides a comprehensive framework for understanding human goals and motivations in Hindu philosophy. This chapter explores how these four aims of life can be applied to economic activities and decision-making, offering a holistic approach to balancing material pursuits with ethical and spiritual considerations.

Dharma (Righteousness) in Business Decisions

The ethical basis for all human endeavors, including monetary ambitions, is dharma, which is sometimes translated as duty or righteousness. Dharma, as applied to corporate choices, emphasizes doing the right thing and meeting one's obligations to different groups of people.

All economic actions should be conducted ethically, according to the notion of dharma in business. Among these include being forthright in all dealings, treating others fairly, and making prudent use of resources. The Manusmriti is a law treatise from ancient India that lays forth principles for how one should act in all facets of economic life. It stresses the significance of being truthful, honest, and fair while dealing with money.

When making business decisions in accordance with dharma, one must think about how their activities will affect the world at large. This is in line with stakeholder theory and contemporary ideas of corporate social responsibility. Considerations like as employee welfare, community impact, and environmental sustainability would be high on the list of priorities for a dharma-driven company leader.

Businesses are also encouraged by the idea of dharma to make sure their actions are in line with what society values and needs. One way to achieve this is to embrace business models that provide shared benefit for all parties involved, or to design goods and services that solve urgent social or environmental problems. In practice, dharma-driven business decisions might include:

1. Implementing fair labor practices and ensuring safe working conditions
2. Adopting transparent and ethical pricing strategies
3. Investing in environmentally sustainable technologies and practices
4. Engaging in philanthropic activities that benefit the wider community
5. Prioritizing long-term sustainability over short-term profit maximization

By incorporating dharma into business decisions, organizations can build trust with stakeholders, enhance their reputation, and contribute to the overall well-being of society. This approach recognizes that businesses are not isolated entities but integral parts of the social and ecological systems in which they operate.

Artha (Wealth) as a Means, Not an End

According to Hindu thought, achieving artha, or material prosperity, is a worthy aim for every human being. Having said that, keep in mind that artha is not an aim in itself but rather a tool to be used in the performance of one's obligations.

Individual and societal financial security is a fundamental aspect of artha. As such, it acknowledges that achieving dharma and higher spiritual aims requires a specific degree of financial wealth. But one's moral behavior and spiritual development should not suffer for the sake of material gain.

When it comes to money, seeing artha as a tool instead of a goal promotes a more sustainable and balanced way to make and spend money. It casts doubt on the boundless spending and accumulation that permeates contemporary economic theory.

A well-rounded strategy for artha is laid forth in the ancient

Indian book Arthashastra, which deals with economic policy and statecraft. The author of Arthashastra, Kautilya, contends that the other purusharthas rest on artha. He argues that it becomes impossible to seek moral life (dharma) and sensual pleasure (kama) in the absence of society and individual wealth and security. While material riches is important, Kautilya warns against putting it ahead of dharma and kama.

Practical applications of viewing artha as a means rather than an end might include:

1. Focusing on value creation rather than mere profit extraction
2. Investing in sustainable and socially responsible business practices
3. Prioritizing employee well-being and development alongside financial performance
4. Engaging in philanthropic activities and social entrepreneurship
5. Adopting circular economy principles to maximize resource efficiency

This approach to artha aligns with modern concepts of sustainable development and inclusive growth. It recognizes that true prosperity cannot be measured solely in financial terms but must also consider social and environmental impacts.

Kama (Desire) and Conscious Consumption

The third purushartha, kama, which means desire or pleasure, is a major influence on monetary conduct, especially in regard to consumption habits. Kama, in the context of economic life, is the impulse that motivates people to seek out material goods and satisfy their needs.

Although it is acknowledged that kama is a natural part of being human, Hindu thought stresses the significance of self-control and deliberate pursuit of one's wants. Many modern economies are plagued by consumerism and overconsumption, yet this viewpoint gives useful insights on how to overcome these issues.

There should be moderation in one's spending habits, according to the Buddhist economic paradigm, which is similar to Hindu thought. Renouncing the competitive economy in favor of a cooperative approach, it demands meeting needs without indulging greed. This is in line with the idea of conscious consumerism, in which people choose their purchases and consumption patterns with intention.

Applying the principle of kama to economic life involves:

1. Distinguishing between genuine needs and artificially created wants
2. Promoting mindfulness and contentment in consumption patterns
3. Encouraging the development of products and services that provide meaningful value rather than merely stimulating desires
4. Addressing the psychological and emotional aspects of consumption

Research on green consumption behaviors provides insights into how desires can be channeled towards more sustainable outcomes. A study on sustainable food consumption in the U.S. found that personal norms, associated with affective and evaluative mechanisms, play a salient role in shaping green consumption desires. This suggests that appealing to personal values and emotions can be effective in promoting more conscious consumption patterns.

Practical strategies for promoting conscious consumption might include:

1. Education programs that raise awareness about the environmental and social impacts of consumption choices
2. Marketing approaches that emphasize quality, durability, and sustainability over novelty and status

3. Policy measures that incentivize sustainable consumption patterns

4. Business models that prioritize service and experience over material ownership

By encouraging a more mindful approach to kama in economic life, it is possible to address the excesses of consumerism while still acknowledging the role of desire and pleasure in human experience.

Moksha (Liberation) and Economic Detachment

In Hindu philosophy, moksha, which means liberation or release, is the pinnacle of human life. The notion of moksha sheds light on the origins of prosperity, achievement, and contentment as they pertain to monetary matters.

Moksha is the liberation from ignorance and the reincarnation cycle. Moksha means "self-knowledge," "self-actualization," and "self-realization" in the psychological and epistemological dimensions. The economic world is typically dominated by materialistic ideas of success and fulfillment, but this view of moksha contradicts them.

Not in the sense of ignoring one's obligations in this world, but rather in order to keep a larger view of what it means to be wealthy and successful, the pursuit of moksha promotes some distancing from financial concerns. This distancing can lessen the impulse for wasteful acquisition and consumption, which in turn can lead to more moral and environmentally responsible economic practices.

"Action with renunciation" or "craving-free, dharma-driven action" (Nishkam Karma) is presented in the Bhagavad Gita, and the idea of moksha in economic life is in line with it. One should participate in economic activities not for the sake of one's own fortune or fame, but rather as a matter of moral obligation and the common good, according to this view.

Practical applications of moksha-oriented thinking in economic life might include:

1. Adopting a stakeholder approach to business that considers the well-being of all affected parties
2. Prioritizing long-term sustainability over short-term profit maximization
3. Investing in employee well-being and personal development
4. Engaging in philanthropic activities and social entrepreneurship
5. Promoting work-life balance and opportunities for spiritual growth within organizations

"Giving" rather than "having" in material terms is likewise related to moksha. According to the Buddhist economic model, this necessitates a change in mindset from one focused on material gain and possessions to one that values giving up what one has and instead working together in harmony and peace.

The quest of moksha does not often include giving up all economic activity, however it is an essential point to remember. Instead, it promotes a more measured and conscientious way of making and spending money. It is possible to attain spiritual freedom while still participating in worldly pursuits, according to the Vedantic doctrine of jivanmukti (liberation in this life).

A thorough foundation for comprehending and directing monetary life is provided by the four Purusharthas: Dharma, Artha, Kama, and Moksha. More ethical, sustainable, and satisfying methods of producing and consuming wealth as well as organizing the economy as a whole can be achieved by incorporating these values into economic decision-making and behavior.

This all-encompassing view acknowledges the significance of artha, or material wealth, and the function of kama, or wants, in economic life, while also stressing the necessity of dharma, or ethical behavior, and keeping a larger view of the nature of success and satisfaction, or moksha. It presents an alternative, more holistic, and long-term plan for economic development, rejecting the reductionist emphasis on increasing profits and gross domestic product that dominates contemporary economic theory.

Major changes in consumer habits, corporate strategies, and government spending plans would be necessary to put these ideas into action. Yet, in light of the growing urgency of global issues like climate change, inequality, and social fragmentation, the Purusharthas' wisdom might help us rethink our economic systems to ensure financial and spiritual prosperity.

Incorporating these four goals into our economic actions may help us build economies that do more than just make money; they can encourage moral conduct, provide for basic human necessities, and aid in the personal and societal emancipation of all people.

References:
1. https://indiafoundation.in/articles-and-commentaries/buddhist-economics-of-compassion-and-communion/
2. https://www.newswise.com/articles/understanding-the-desire-for-green-consumption-norms-emotions-and-attitudes
3. https://encyclopedia.pub/entry/29371
4. https://www.paramporulfoundation.com/how-can-money-and-moksha-unveil-lifes-truths-and-purpose/
5. https://en.wikipedia.org/wiki/Moksha

Chapter 5: Karma Economics: Action and Consequence

Karma, a central idea in Eastern philosophies, provides a useful framework for thinking about the link between our deeds and the results we get. Applying this age-old knowledge to modern economic situations yields rich insights into ethical decision-making, long-term strategy, and environmentally responsible company operations. Corporate social responsibility (CSR) and long-term planning in company strategy are two examples of karmic actions discussed in this chapter, which also examines the relevance of karmic principles to economic operations.

Understanding the Law of Karma in Economic Contexts

Both Hinduism and Buddhism center on the tenet of "what goes around comes around," or the law of karma. Every action has immediate and long-term implications that impact future experiences; this is the core of karma. This idea promotes a more comprehensive and moral approach to conducting business when applied to economic situations.

Karma, as it pertains to the corporate world, is that our deeds have consequences that follow us wherever we go in our careers. Our businesses' futures are shaped by the choices we make, the honesty we maintain, and the value we provide. The reputation, client connections, and chances for our firm are all improved when we act positively, because good things tend to attract good things.

This karmic view is congruent with contemporary ideas about corporate social responsibility and environmentally friendly procedures. It seems to imply that doing what's unethical will hurt the company in the long run, even if it helps in the near run. On the flip side, doing the right thing and making a constructive impact on society are viewed as investments that will pay off in the long run.

The application of karmic principles in business encourages:
1. Ethical decision-making: Recognizing that actions have consequences promotes integrity and fairness in business practices.
2. Accountability and responsibility: Karma emphasizes personal responsibility, encouraging managers to carefully consider the impact of their decisions.
3. Long-term perspective: Understanding that actions have long-term consequences aligns with sustainable business practices and strategic planning.
4. Positive organizational culture: Leading by example and demonstrating ethical behavior creates an environment of mutual respect and accountability.
5. Enhanced relationships: Approaching business relationships with authenticity and a genuine desire to support others builds stronger, more trusting connections.

The karmic approach to business also resonates with the concept of "dharma" or duty in Hindu philosophy. In the context of business, dharma encourages individuals to fulfill their responsibilities not just for personal gain, but for the greater good of society. This aligns with modern ideas of corporate social responsibility and stakeholder capitalism.

Long-term Thinking in Business Strategy

The principle of karma naturally encourages long-term thinking in business strategy. By recognizing that today's actions shape future outcomes, businesses are motivated to consider the broader and more distant implications of their decisions.

Long-term thinking in business involves several key aspects:
1. Vision and goal-setting: Long-term thinking begins with a clear vision of where the company wants to be in the future. This involves setting long-term goals that guide decisions, investments, and overall strategy.

2. Sustainable growth: Rather than focusing on short-term profits, long-term thinking emphasizes sustainable, incremental growth. This might involve investing in areas where immediate returns are not evident but long-term success is built, such as research, employee development, and organizational structures.

3. Risk management: Long-term thinking involves proactively considering potential risks and developing strategies to manage them. This makes companies more adaptable and resilient in the face of change.

4. Innovation and creativity: A long-term perspective allows businesses to invest in innovation and creativity, which can lead to unique developments and competitive advantages.

The benefits of adopting a long-term perspective in business strategy are numerous:

1. Enhanced decision-making: Long-term thinking encourages decisions based on future impact rather than short-term outcomes, leading to more deliberate commitments and reduced risk.

2. Clear direction for growth: Setting long-term goals provides alignment across the company, creating a space for better planning and execution.

3. Competitive advantage: A long-term approach allows businesses to invest in innovation and keep up with technological advancements, helping them remain competitive in an ever-evolving environment.

4. Consistent performance: By focusing on sustainable, incremental growth over short-term wins, businesses can achieve more consistent performance over time.

5. Improved returns: While immediate financial gains might not be realized, long-term profit maximization often leads to higher returns over time. This stable and reliable growth can also attract long-term investors.

6. Talent attraction and retention: Investing in long-term goals

often includes investing in employee development, which can increase employee retention and improve overall workplace culture.

7. Increased adaptability: A long-term strategy that includes risk management makes businesses more resilient to unforeseen challenges and changes.

8. Enhanced sustainability: Long-term thinking allows businesses to focus on social responsibility and implement sustainable practices, aligning with environmental and societal goals.

The karmic perspective reinforces these benefits by emphasizing the interconnectedness of actions and outcomes over time. It encourages businesses to consider not just the immediate effects of their decisions, but also the potential ripple effects that may manifest in the future.

Corporate Social Responsibility as Karmic Action
One way of looking at corporate social responsibility (CSR) is as an example of how karmic principles are put into practice in the business sector. Companies engage in corporate social responsibility (CSR) when they implement policies and programs as part of their corporate governance framework to make sure their business practices are good for society and ethical.

Sustainable operations in all three areas (financial, social, and environmental) are important to corporate social responsibility (CSR). This fits in nicely with the karmic idea that doing good deeds benefits the company and the world at large.

CSR initiatives generally fall into four categories:

1. Environmental responsibility: Initiatives aimed at reducing pollution, greenhouse gas emissions, and promoting sustainable use of natural resources.

2. Human rights responsibility: Providing fair labor practices, fair trade practices, and disavowing child labor.

3. Philanthropic responsibility: Funding educational programs,

supporting health initiatives, donating to causes, and supporting community beautification projects.

4. Economic responsibility: Improving business operations while participating in sustainable practices.

From a karmic perspective, these CSR initiatives can be seen as positive actions that will yield beneficial consequences for the business over time. The business benefits of CSR include:

1. Enhanced corporate reputation and brand equity.
2. Increased customer loyalty and engagement.
3. Operational cost savings through improved efficiencies.
4. Improved employee retention and commitment.
5. Increased investor support.
6. Better relationships with regulatory bodies.

Businesses are encouraged to see CSR as an essential part of their operations, rather as a separate campaign or public relations effort, by the idea of karma. It implies that businesses may reap the benefits of good karma by continuously doing what's best for society and the environment.

Businesses that share this view include Starbucks, which has made corporate social responsibility (CSR) an integral part of its operations. Ethical sourcing procedures, environmental protection, and community engagement are some of Starbucks' CSR activities. In addition to improving Starbucks' image and fostering consumer loyalty, these initiatives have a positive impact on society and the environment.

The idea of "having" in economic life is at odds with the karmic approach to corporate social responsibility, which emphasizes "giving" instead. According to the Buddhist economic model, this necessitates a change in mindset from one focused on material gain and possessions to one that values giving up what one has and instead working together in harmony and peace. The core of both karmic economics and contemporary CSR practices is this change in emphasis from maximizing short-term profits to creating value for all stakeholders in the long run.

A robust foundation for encouraging sustainable, socially responsible, and ethical business activities may be found in the economic application of karmic principles. Businesses are motivated to think about the long-term effects of their activities when they grasp the economic concept of karma. This leads to more responsible and considerate decision-making.

Strategic planning with an eye on the future, informed by karmic principles, fosters creativity, resilience, and long-term growth. In doing so, it urges companies to think about their long-term effects on people and the planet, not just their bottom line.

Considering CSR via the karma lens transforms it from a collection of programs into a way of doing business that prioritizes the well-being of both society and corporations. Businesses may contribute to their own success and longevity by operating in ways that benefit all stakeholders. This is called positive karma.

With the world's problems become ever more complicated, the teachings of karmic economics can help us find better ways to organize our economic systems so that they are more ethical, sustainable, and satisfying. Businesses that adopt these values will be better able to help the economy thrive while also improving people's lives and the planet. This will lead to a win-win situation.

References

1. Goudarzi, S., Knowles, E. D., & Badaan, V. (2022). Neoliberal policies, institutions have prompted preference for greater income inequality. NYU. https://www.nyu.edu/about/news-publications/news/2022/may/neoliberal-policies--institutions-have-prompted-preference-for-g.html
2. Kumar, R. (n.d.). Karma Theory and it's Importance in Business. LinkedIn. https://www.linkedin.com/pulse/karma-theory-its-importance-business-rajesh-kumar
3. EZRA coaching. (2024). The Power of Long-Term

Thinking in Business. https://helloezra.com/resources/insights/long-term-thinking-business

4. The Intact One. (2024). Concept of Karma, Meaning and Importance to Managers. https://theintactone.com/2024/09/07/concept-of-karma-meaning-and-importance-to-managers/

5. Muniapan, B., & Raj, S.J. (2014). Corporate Social Responsibility Communication from the Vedantic, Dharmic and Karmic Perspectives. In Communicating Corporate Social Responsibility: Perspectives and Practice (Critical Studies on Corporate Responsibility, Governance and Sustainability, Vol. 6, pp. 337-354). Emerald Group Publishing Limited. https://doi.org/10.1108/S2043-9059(2014)0000006001

6. Tupil, N. N. (n.d.). Karma, is it relevant for companies and business leaders? LinkedIn. https://www.linkedin.com/pulse/karma-relevant-companies-business-leaders-nash-narasimhan-tupil

7. Corporate Finance Institute. (n.d.). Corporate Social Responsibility (CSR) - Types and Business Benefits. https://corporatefinanceinstitute.com/resources/esg/corporate-social-responsibility-csr/

Chapter 6: Ethical Leadership in the Dharmic Economy

The concept of ethical leadership in the context of a dharmic economy represents a paradigm shift in how we approach business management and organizational governance. This chapter explores the cultivation of wisdom and compassion in leadership, decision-making based on dharmic principles, and examines case studies of dharmic leaders in modern business.

Cultivating Wisdom and Compassion in Leadership

Wisdom and compassion, according to the dharmic view, are not only admirable qualities in a leader, but necessary for their success. The significance of emotional intelligence and ethical conduct in organizational performance is becoming more acknowledged in recent studies on effective leadership, which is in line with this approach.

Being a wise leader means you can assess events, people, and the outcomes in the long run, and then make decisions and judgments accordingly. A comprehensive comprehension of interdependence and the wider consequences of one's deeds is wisdom in the dharmic setting, which extends beyond merely intellectual understanding.

Conversely, empathy and a true care for other people's welfare are at the heart of compassion. A compassionate leader prioritizes the well-being of all parties impacted by the organization's decisions, including workers, stakeholders, and the community at large.

Leaders that are both wise and compassionate are described by Hougaard and Carter as having "Wise Compassion." They contend that leaders who display both compassion and knowledge have a far greater beneficial effect on staff wellbeing and productivity than leaders who display just one of these traits alone.

To cultivate wisdom and compassion, leaders can adopt several practices:

1. Mindfulness and Self-Reflection: Regular meditation and self-reflection practices can help leaders develop greater self-awareness and emotional regulation.
2. Continuous Learning: Engaging in ongoing education and exposure to diverse perspectives can broaden a leader's understanding and decision-making capacity.
3. Empathy Training: Structured programs to develop empathy can enhance a leader's ability to understand and relate to others' experiences.
4. Ethical Decision-Making Frameworks: Implementing frameworks that incorporate ethical considerations into the decision-making process can help leaders navigate complex situations.
5. Servant Leadership: Adopting a servant leadership approach, where the primary focus is on serving others, can naturally cultivate both wisdom and compassion.

The cultivation of these qualities aligns with the dharmic concept of "citta-shuddhi" or purification of consciousness, which is considered essential for effective leadership.

Decision-making Based on Dharmic Principles

Decision-making in a dharmic economy goes beyond traditional cost-benefit analysis to incorporate a broader set of considerations. This approach recognizes the multidimensional nature of business decisions and their far-reaching impacts.

Key dharmic principles that can guide decision-making include:
1. Interconnectedness: Recognizing that all actions have ripple effects throughout the organization and broader society.
2. Long-term Perspective: Considering the long-term consequences of decisions rather than focusing solely on short-

term gains.
3. Ethical Conduct: Ensuring that decisions align with ethical principles and contribute to the greater good.
4. Sustainability: Prioritizing decisions that promote environmental and social sustainability.
5. Stakeholder Consideration: Taking into account the interests of all stakeholders, not just shareholders.
6. Balance: Striving for balance between economic, social, and environmental objectives.

The dharmic approach to decision-making also emphasizes the importance of the decision-maker's qualities. As noted in research on decision-making from a dharmic perspective, "the dharmic way recognizes how the qualities of the decision-maker impact the decisions and hence lays emphasis on the refinement of these qualities".

Practical strategies for implementing dharmic decision-making include:
1. Multistakeholder Consultation: Engaging with diverse stakeholders to understand the full range of impacts and perspectives.
2. Scenario Planning: Considering multiple potential outcomes and their long-term implications.
3. Ethical Impact Assessment: Conducting formal assessments of the ethical implications of major decisions.
4. Mindfulness Practices: Incorporating mindfulness techniques to enhance clarity and reduce bias in decision-making.
5. Value Alignment: Ensuring that decisions align with the organization's core values and ethical principles.

By adopting these approaches, leaders can make decisions that not only drive business success but also contribute positively to society and the environment.

Case Studies of Dharmic Leaders in Modern Business

While the concept of dharmic leadership may seem abstract, there are numerous examples of leaders who have successfully applied these principles in modern business contexts. These case studies demonstrate how dharmic leadership can drive both ethical conduct and business success.

Case Study 1: Ratan Tata - Tata Group

Ratan Tata, the former chairman of Tata Group, exemplifies many aspects of dharmic leadership. Under his guidance, the Tata Group maintained a strong commitment to ethical business practices and social responsibility while achieving significant business growth.

Key dharmic leadership principles demonstrated by Ratan Tata include:

1. Long-term Vision: Tata consistently prioritized long-term sustainability over short-term profits.

2. Ethical Conduct: The Tata Group is renowned for its commitment to ethical business practices, even in challenging environments.

3. Social Responsibility: Tata has invested heavily in social initiatives, including education and healthcare programs for underserved communities.

4. Stakeholder Consideration: Tata's leadership style considered the interests of employees, communities, and the environment alongside shareholder interests.

Case Study 2: Satya Nadella - Microsoft

Since becoming CEO of Microsoft in 2014, Satya Nadella has demonstrated many qualities of dharmic leadership, transforming the company's culture and strategic direction.

Nadella's approach includes:

1. Empathy and Compassion: Nadella has emphasized the importance of empathy in leadership and product development.

2. Growth Mindset: Encouraging continuous learning and

adaptation throughout the organization.

3. Sustainability Focus: Under Nadella's leadership, Microsoft has made significant commitments to environmental sustainability.

4. Inclusive Leadership: Promoting diversity and inclusion as core values within the organization.

Case Study 3: Anita Roddick - The Body Shop

The late Anita Roddick, founder of The Body Shop, was a pioneer in ethical business practices and dharmic leadership principles.

Roddick's leadership embodied:

1. Ethical Sourcing: Implementing fair trade practices and ethical sourcing long before they became industry norms.
2. Environmental Stewardship: Promoting environmentally friendly products and practices.
3. Social Activism: Using the business as a platform for social and environmental activism.
4. Stakeholder Value: Prioritizing value creation for all stakeholders, including suppliers, employees, and communities.

These case studies demonstrate that dharmic leadership principles can be successfully applied in various business contexts, leading to both ethical conduct and business success. They show how leaders can balance profit motives with broader societal and environmental considerations, creating value for all stakeholders.

References

1. Hougaard, R., & Carter, J. (n.d.). Wise Compassionate Leadership. Potential Project. https://www.potentialproject.com/wise-compassionate-leadership
2. Kalagnanam, S. (2022). Research finds principles of dharma as a basis for developing sustainable and responsible business. Edwards School of Business, University of Saskatchewan. https://

www.edwards.usask.ca/news/2022/research-finds-principles-of-dharma-as-a-basis-for-developing-sustainable-and-responsible-business.aspx
3. Radhakrishnan, R., & Jha, S. (n.d.). Approaching Decision-Making from a Dharmic Perspective. Purushartha: A Journal of Management Ethics and Spirituality. http://journals.smsvaranasi.com/index.php/purushartha/article/view/278
4. Srivastava, A. (2024). Dharmic Leadership for Tackling Grand Challenges. AACSB Insights. https://www.aacsb.edu/insights/articles/2024/01/dharmic-leadership-for-tackling-grand-challenges

Chapter 7: Conscious Capitalism: A Dharmic Approach

The concept of conscious capitalism, when viewed through a dharmic lens, offers a compelling framework for creating businesses that balance profit with purpose and social responsibility. This chapter explores how stakeholder theory can be enriched by dharmic principles, examines purpose-driven business models, and discusses strategies for balancing profit with social and environmental impact.

Stakeholder Theory through a Dharmic Lens

According to R. Edward Freeman's stakeholder theory, businesses shouldn't limit themselves to making decisions based on the interests and consequences of their shareholders alone. This idea gains more complexity and moral weight when seen via a dharmic prism.

Principles central to stakeholder theory are congruent with the dharmic worldview, which places an emphasis on interdependence and interconnection. According to studies on dharmic decision-making, "the dharmic way recognizes how the qualities of the decision-maker impact the decisions and hence lays emphasis on the refinement of these qualities." That is... There is a stronger ethical need to consider stakeholders in a dharmic framework, as this goes beyond simple strategic calculation.

Key aspects of stakeholder theory through a dharmic lens include:

1. Expanded Notion of Stakeholders: The dharmic view encourages businesses to consider not just immediate stakeholders but also the broader community, environment, and even future generations in their decision-making processes.

2. Ethical Dimension: Stakeholder engagement is seen not just as a means to an end but as an ethical duty. The concept of dharma emphasizes performing one's duties in accordance with one's position and standing in society.

3. Long-term Perspective: The dharmic approach to stakeholder theory encourages businesses to consider the long-term consequences of their actions, aligning with the concept of karma.

4. Holistic Value Creation: Rather than focusing solely on financial value, a dharmic approach to stakeholder theory emphasizes creating value across multiple dimensions - economic, social, environmental, and spiritual.

Implementing stakeholder theory through a dharmic lens might involve:

1. Stakeholder Mapping: Developing comprehensive stakeholder maps that include broader societal and environmental considerations.

2. Ethical Decision-Making Frameworks: Incorporating dharmic principles into decision-making processes to ensure ethical considerations are at the forefront.

3. Stakeholder Engagement: Developing deep, meaningful relationships with stakeholders based on principles of mutual respect and interdependence.

4. Impact Assessment: Regularly assessing the impact of business decisions on all stakeholders, including those often overlooked in traditional business models.

Purpose-Driven Business Models

An organic development from dharmic ideas used in the corporate sphere is purpose-driven business models. In keeping with the dharmic idea of dharma, or responsibility, these approaches place an emphasis on a greater good rather than monetary gain.

Research indicates that 79% of consumers are more loyal to firms that are purpose-driven, thus highlighting the relevance of purpose in business. Purposes should be genuine, based on the organization's principles, and intended to make a beneficial difference in society from a dharmic viewpoint.

Key elements of purpose-driven business models from a dharmic perspective include:
1. Authentic Purpose: The purpose should be deeply connected to the heart of the organization, personal, and authentic. It should answer the fundamental question of why the company exists beyond making money.
2. Alignment with Dharma: The purpose should align with the concept of dharma, which encompasses performing one's duties and responsibilities in a way that contributes to the greater good.
3. Stakeholder Value Creation: Purpose-driven models should aim to create value for all stakeholders, not just shareholders, reflecting the dharmic principle of interconnectedness.

4. Integration of Purpose and Strategy: The purpose should be fully integrated into the organization's strategy, operations, and decision-making processes.

5. Long-term Orientation: Purpose-driven models should take a long-term view, considering the lasting impact of business decisions on society and the environment.

Implementing a purpose-driven business model might involve:
1. Purpose Discovery: Engaging in a deep, reflective process to uncover the organization's authentic purpose, often by revisiting why the company was created and what problem it is trying to solve.
2. Purpose Integration: Embedding the purpose into every aspect of the business, from strategy and operations to culture and employee engagement.
3. Measurement and Accountability: Developing metrics to measure progress towards purpose-related goals and holding the organization accountable for achieving them.

4. Stakeholder Engagement: Actively engaging with stakeholders to ensure the purpose remains relevant and impactful.

5. Continuous Evolution: Regularly revisiting and refining the purpose to ensure it remains aligned with societal needs and the organization's capabilities.

Balancing Profit with Social and Environmental Impact

The dharmic approach to business recognizes the importance of profit but views it as a means to fulfill one's duties and responsibilities rather than an end in itself. This perspective offers valuable insights for balancing profit with social and environmental impact.

The concept of "artha" in dharmic philosophy acknowledges the importance of material prosperity but emphasizes that it should be pursued ethically and in balance with other life goals. This aligns with the modern notion of the triple bottom line - people, planet, and profit.

Key principles for balancing profit with social and environmental impact from a dharmic perspective include:

1. Ethical Wealth Creation: Wealth should be created through ethical means, avoiding exploitation and harm to others or the environment.

2. Stakeholder Value: Business success should be measured not just in terms of financial profit but in the value created for all stakeholders.

3. Long-term Perspective: Decisions should consider long-term impacts, recognizing the karmic consequences of business actions.

4. Moderation: The pursuit of profit should be balanced with other considerations, avoiding extremes of greed or neglect of financial sustainability.

5. Regenerative Practices: Business practices should aim to regenerate rather than deplete social and environmental resources.

Strategies for implementing this balance might include:

1. Integrated Reporting: Adopting integrated reporting frameworks that consider financial, social, and environmental performance.

2. Impact Investment: Prioritizing investments that generate both financial returns and positive social or environmental impact.

3. Circular Economy Models: Implementing circular economy principles to minimize waste and environmental impact.

4. Employee Well-being Programs: Investing in programs that promote employee well-being and development, recognizing the interconnectedness of individual and organizational success.

5. Community Engagement: Actively engaging with and contributing to local communities, recognizing the business's role in the broader social fabric.

6. Environmental Stewardship: Implementing robust environmental management systems and setting ambitious sustainability goals.

Case Studies

Several companies have successfully implemented aspects of conscious capitalism through a dharmic lens:

1. Patagonia: The outdoor clothing company has long been a leader in purpose-driven business, with a mission to "use business to inspire and implement solutions to the environmental crisis". Their commitment to environmental stewardship, fair labor practices, and transparency aligns closely with dharmic principles.

2. Tata Group: Under the leadership of Ratan Tata, the Indian conglomerate has demonstrated a strong commitment to ethical business practices and social responsibility, reflecting many aspects of dharmic leadership.

3. Grameen Bank: Founded by Muhammad Yunus, Grameen Bank's microfinance model exemplifies a purpose-driven approach that balances profit with social impact, aligning with dharmic principles of ethical wealth creation and stakeholder value.

Conscious capitalism, when viewed through a dharmic lens, offers a powerful framework for creating businesses that are both profitable and socially responsible. By applying dharmic principles to stakeholder theory, developing authentic purpose-driven models, and balancing profit with social and environmental impact, businesses can create lasting value for all stakeholders while contributing to the greater good.

As we face increasingly complex global challenges, this approach to business offers a path forward that aligns economic success with ethical conduct and societal well-being. It challenges businesses to look beyond short-term profits and consider their broader role in society, fostering a more sustainable and equitable economic system.

The implementation of these principles requires a fundamental shift in how we think about business and its role in society. It calls for leaders who can balance multiple stakeholder interests, make decisions with long-term consequences in mind, and maintain an unwavering commitment to ethical conduct. While challenging, the potential rewards - both for businesses and society at large - are immense.

As we move forward, further research and practical experimentation will be crucial in refining and implementing these concepts. By continuing to explore the intersection of dharmic principles and modern business practices, we can develop more robust models of conscious capitalism that are capable of addressing the complex challenges of the 21st century.

References

1. Radhakrishnan, R., & Jha, S. (n.d.). Approaching Decision-Making from a Dharmic Perspective. Purushartha: A Journal of Management Ethics and Spirituality. http://journals.smsvaranasi.com/index.php/purushartha/article/view/278
2. Swarajya. (n.d.). Hindunomics: From State To Wealth To Dharma To Happiness. https://swarajyamag.com/magazine/hindunomics-from-state-to-wealth-to-dharma-to-happiness
3. Srivastava, A. (2024). Dharmic Leadership for Tackling Grand Challenges. AACSB Insights. https://www.aacsb.edu/insights/articles/2024/01/dharmic-leadership-for-tackling-grand-challenges
4. Reframing Our Purpose Through Dharma - AACSB. (n.d.). https://www.aacsb.edu/insights/articles/2023/08/reframing-our-purpose-through-dharma
5. Hudson, K. (n.d.). Driven by a purpose: how to create a purpose-driven business model. AMBA. https://www.amba-bga.com/insights/driven-by-a-purpose-how-to-create-a-purpose-driven-business-model
6. Quirk's Media. (n.d.). How to create and maintain a purpose-driven business. https://www.quirks.com/articles/how-to-create-and-maintain-a-purpose-driven-business

Chapter 8: Sustainable Business Practices

Companies in today's global economy are realizing the importance of sustainable practices to strike a balance between profit and social and environmental responsibility. Case studies of sustainable dharmic firms are presented, and the chapter delves into how businesses might incorporate environmental stewardship into their operations. It also investigates circular economy notions through the prism of dharmic thinking.

Integrating Environmental Stewardship in Business Operations

The term "environmental stewardship" describes those who make an effort to preserve and use the world's natural resources in a sustainable way. A comprehensive strategy that takes into account the environmental effect of a company's actions is necessary to integrate environmental responsibility into its operations.

Environmental audits are an important first step in environmental stewardship since they allow you to evaluate your present procedures and find places where you can make improvements. Businesses may benefit from this audit by learning how to develop SMART objectives that are in line with environmental stewardship principles: precise, measurable, achievable, relevant, and time-bound.

Key areas for integrating environmental stewardship include:

1. Energy efficiency: Implementing energy-efficient technologies and practices can significantly reduce a company's carbon footprint and operational costs. This may involve upgrading to energy-efficient equipment, optimizing building

systems, and utilizing renewable energy sources like solar or wind power.

2. Waste reduction and recycling: Implementing comprehensive waste management strategies, including recycling programs and waste reduction initiatives, can minimize environmental impact and potentially create new revenue streams through resource recovery.

3. Sustainable sourcing: Adopting responsible sourcing practices that consider the environmental and social impact of suppliers and materials can help reduce overall environmental footprint and promote sustainability throughout the supply chain.

4. Water conservation: Implementing water-saving technologies and practices, such as low-flow fixtures and water recycling systems, can reduce water consumption and associated costs.

5. Green product development: Designing products with environmental considerations in mind, such as using sustainable materials, improving energy efficiency, and enhancing recyclability, can create competitive advantages and meet growing consumer demand for eco-friendly products.

6. Employee engagement: Educating and engaging employees in environmental initiatives can foster a culture of sustainability within the organization and drive innovation in sustainable practices.

7. Stakeholder collaboration: Engaging with suppliers, customers, and other stakeholders to promote shared commitment to environmental stewardship can lead to innovative solutions and greater impact.

Integrating environmental stewardship into business operations not only contributes to environmental preservation but also offers numerous benefits for organizations:

1. Cost savings: By implementing energy-efficient technologies, reducing waste, and optimizing resource usage, companies can reduce their operational costs.
2. Enhanced reputation: Demonstrating a commitment to environmental stewardship can improve brand image and attract environmentally conscious consumers and investors.
3. Regulatory compliance: Proactively incorporating sustainable practices helps companies stay compliant with environmental regulations and mitigate potential risks associated with non-compliance.
4. Innovation and competitive advantage: Investing in sustainable technologies and practices can drive innovation and create new market opportunities.
5. Employee satisfaction and retention: A strong commitment to environmental stewardship can improve employee morale, attract top talent, and increase retention rates.

Circular Economy Concepts in Dharmic Thought

The circular economy is an economic model that aims to eliminate waste and maximize resource efficiency by keeping products, components, and materials at their highest utility and value at all times. This concept aligns closely with dharmic principles of interconnectedness, balance, and responsible resource use.

Several key concepts from dharmic thought resonate with circular economy principles:
1. Ahimsa (non-harming): The principle of ahimsa extends beyond non-violence towards living beings to encompass non-harm to the environment. This aligns with the circular economy's goal of minimizing environmental impact through reduced waste and pollution.
2. Vasudhaiva Kutumbakam (the world is one family): This concept emphasizes the interconnectedness of all living beings and promotes a sense of responsibility towards the planet's well-

being. In circular economy terms, this translates to recognizing the interconnected nature of economic activities and their impact on the environment.

3. Reincarnation and rebirth: The cyclical nature of life in dharmic traditions parallels the circular economy's emphasis on continuous cycles of use, recovery, and regeneration of resources.

4. Ayurveda (balanced living): Ayurvedic principles of balance and harmony between individuals and their environment align with the circular economy's focus on creating systems that are restorative and regenerative by design.

5. Dharmic responsibility: The concept of dharma, or moral duty, can be extended to include responsibility towards the environment. This aligns with the circular economy's emphasis on businesses taking responsibility for the entire lifecycle of their products.

These dharmic principles provide a philosophical foundation for implementing circular economy practices in business. By viewing economic activities through this lens, businesses can develop more holistic and sustainable approaches to resource use and waste management.

Case Studies of Sustainable Dharmic Businesses

Several businesses have successfully integrated dharmic principles and sustainable practices into their operations. Here are a few notable examples:

1. Patagonia:
While not explicitly dharmic, Patagonia's business practices align closely with dharmic principles of environmental stewardship and social responsibility. The company has implemented numerous sustainable initiatives, including:

- Using recycled materials in their products
- Implementing a repair and reuse program to extend

product lifespans
- Donating 1% of sales to environmental causes
- Encouraging consumers to buy only what they need through their "Don't Buy This Jacket" campaign

Patagonia's approach demonstrates how businesses can prioritize environmental stewardship while maintaining profitability and brand loyalty.

2. Interface:
Interface, a global modular carpet manufacturer, has successfully incorporated environmental stewardship into its business practices. The company's sustainability initiatives include:

- Reducing greenhouse gas emissions by 96%
- Diverting over 4 million pounds of waste from landfills
- Implementing a circular economy model for carpet production
- Setting ambitious goals for becoming a carbon-negative company by 2040

Interface's success shows how traditional manufacturing businesses can transform their operations to align with sustainable and circular economy principles.

3. Tata Group:
The Tata Group, an Indian multinational conglomerate, has a long history of integrating dharmic principles into its business practices. Some of their sustainable initiatives include:

- Implementing water conservation and recycling programs across their operations
- Investing in renewable energy projects
- Developing eco-friendly products and services
- Engaging in extensive community development and social welfare programs

The Tata Group's approach demonstrates how large, diverse

businesses can incorporate dharmic principles of social responsibility and environmental stewardship across multiple sectors.

4. Grameen Bank: Founded by Muhammad Yunus, Grameen Bank exemplifies the integration of dharmic principles of social responsibility with sustainable business practices. While not explicitly environmental in focus, Grameen Bank's microfinance model promotes sustainable economic development in rural communities, aligning with dharmic concepts of interconnectedness and balanced growth.

5. Green Acres Farm: This family-run organic farm in rural America demonstrates how small businesses can implement sustainable practices aligned with dharmic principles. Green Acres Farm focuses on:

- Environmentally friendly farming practices, including crop rotation and natural pest control
- Prioritizing soil health and biodiversity
- Producing high-quality organic produce for local and regional markets
- Engaging in community education on sustainable agriculture

The case studies presented here show how companies of all sizes and in all industries may implement sustainable practices and dharmic concepts. These firms show that it's possible to make money and help the environment by putting an emphasis on social responsibility, environmental protection, and long-term viability.

Sustainable business methods, guided by dharmic values and ideas from the circular economy, provide a strong foundation for making companies that care about the environment and make money. Reducing their ecological footprint, mitigating risks, and creating long-term value for all stakeholders may be achieved by businesses through the adoption of environmental stewardship principles.

A philosophical basis for executing circular economy activities may be found in the dharmic worldview, which places a focus on interdependence, harmony, and accountability. This method pushes companies to think about how their activities will affect the world at large and to aim for practices that are regenerative instead of just sustainable.

Businesses of all sizes and in all industries may benefit from implementing these concepts, as shown in the case studies. Sustainable practices that are in line with dharmic principles may improve environmental consequences, boost brand reputation, and ensure long-term commercial success for businesses of all sizes.

In the face of mounting environmental crises, a more sustainable and regenerative economic system may be achieved via the adoption of sustainable business practices that are informed by dharmic knowledge and the concepts of the circular economy. Businesses may make a significant impact in building a better, more fair future by adopting these practices.

References

1. Technorely. (n.d.). Sustainable Business Practices: Integrating Eco-Friendly Solutions. Retrieved from https://technorely.com/insights/sustainable-business-practices-integrating-eco-friendly-solutions
2. Quirk's Media. (n.d.). How to create and maintain a purpose-driven business. Retrieved from https://www.quirks.com/articles/how-to-create-and-maintain-a-purpose-driven-business
3. Shorts Accountants. (n.d.). Guide to sustainable business practices in 2024. Retrieved from https://blog.shorts.uk.com/sustainable-business-practices
4. Strisutram. (2023, September 27). Sustainability and the Circular Economy: Lessons from Indian Traditions. Retrieved fromhttps://www.strisutram.com/post/sustainability-and-the-circular-

economy-lessons-from-indian-traditions
5. Edwards School of Business, University of Saskatchewan. (2022). Research finds principles of dharma as a basis for developing sustainable and responsible business. Retrieved from https://www.edwards.usask.ca/news/2022/research-finds-principles-of-dharma-as-a-basis-for-developing-sustainable-and-responsible-business.aspx
6. FasterCapital. (n.d.). Case Studies: Successful Examples Of Sustainable Businesses In Rural Communities. Retrieved from https://fastercapital.com/topics/case-studies:-successful-examples-of-sustainable-businesses-in-rural-communities.html
7. FasterCapital. (n.d.). Environmental Stewardship: Integrating Ethics into Business Practices. Retrieved from https://fastercapital.com/content/Environmental-stewardship--Environmental-Stewardship--Integrating-Ethics-into-Business-Practices.html

Chapter 9: Fair Trade and Ethical Supply Chains

In an increasingly interconnected global economy, the principles of fair trade and ethical supply chains have become crucial for businesses aiming to operate responsibly and sustainably. This chapter explores how the concept of ahimsa (non-violence) can be applied to global trade, the importance of ensuring fair wages and working conditions, and the role of transparency and traceability in creating ethical supply chains.

Applying Ahimsa (Non-violence) in Global Trade
The principle of ahimsa, or non-violence, has deep roots in Indian philosophy and was famously championed by Mahatma Gandhi as a means of social and political change. In the context of global trade, ahimsa can be interpreted as a commitment to conducting business in a way that minimizes harm to all stakeholders, including workers, communities, and the environment.

Ahimsa in global trade extends beyond the absence of physical violence to encompass social justice and human rights. It encourages businesses to consider the broader impact of their actions on society and the environment. This holistic approach aligns with modern concepts of corporate social responsibility and sustainable development.

Key aspects of applying ahimsa in global trade include:

1. Ethical sourcing: Ensuring that raw materials and products are obtained in ways that do not exploit workers or damage ecosystems.

2. Fair labor practices: Providing safe working conditions, fair wages, and respecting workers' rights throughout the supply chain.

3. Environmental stewardship: Minimizing the ecological footprint of business operations and promoting sustainable practices.
4. Community engagement: Actively contributing to the well-being of communities affected by business operations.
5. Conflict-free supply chains: Ensuring that business activities do not contribute to violence or conflict in regions where resources are sourced.

Implementing ahimsa in global trade requires a shift in business mindset from short-term profit maximization to long-term value creation for all stakeholders. This approach recognizes the interconnectedness of economic activities and their impact on society and the environment.

Ensuring Fair Wages and Working Conditions

Ensuring fair wages and working conditions is a crucial aspect of ethical supply chains and aligns closely with the principle of ahimsa. Fair compensation and safe working environments not only benefit workers directly but also contribute to economic stability and poverty reduction in communities.

Key elements of ensuring fair wages and working conditions include:

1. Living wages: Paying workers enough to cover basic needs and provide some discretionary income, considering local cost of living and economic conditions.
2. Safe working environments: Implementing robust health and safety measures to protect workers from occupational hazards.
3. Reasonable working hours: Limiting overtime and ensuring adequate rest periods for workers.
4. Freedom of association: Respecting workers' rights to form and join labor unions.
5. Non-discrimination: Ensuring equal opportunities and treatment for all workers regardless of gender, race, or other factors.

6. Elimination of child and forced labor: Implementing strict policies and monitoring systems to prevent exploitation.

A number of businesses have taken the lead in ensuring that their supplier chains adhere to fair labor standards. Take IKEA as an example. They've made a commitment to pay livable wages across their supply chain, taking into account things like local cost of living and family considerations. Over 600,000 employees in IKEA's supply chain have seen salary rises as a result of this program.

In an effort to eradicate forced and child labor, Apple has instituted a stringent supplier evaluation method. The corporation evaluated 1,121 suppliers in 2020, accounting for 94% of total expenditure. Apple has fired 20 vendors for major infractions of its zero-tolerance policy.

In its Global Sourcing Principles and Human Rights Policy, Marks & Spencer (M&S) has established thorough standards for equitable working conditions. In Bangladesh, for example, the Ethical Model Factory initiative has reduced working hours by 42% while keeping or raising salaries, among other improvements to working conditions.

Transparency and Traceability in Supply Chains

Transparency and traceability are essential components of ethical supply chains, enabling businesses and consumers to understand the journey of products from source to shelf. These principles support the application of ahimsa in global trade by making it possible to identify and address potential issues throughout the supply chain.

Supply chain traceability refers to the ability to track the journey of a product and its components throughout the entire supply chain. Implementing traceability systems offers several benefits:

1. Enhanced efficiency: Real-time data and insights enable businesses to identify bottlenecks, reduce waste, and optimize inventory management.

2. Improved accountability: Traceability fosters a culture of responsibility among all supply chain participants.

3. Risk management: Businesses can quickly identify and address potential issues, such as quality control problems or ethical violations.

4. Consumer trust: Transparency builds confidence in products and brands, particularly for ethically-minded consumers.

Technologies enabling supply chain traceability include:

1. Blockchain: Creates an immutable ledger of transactions accessible to all supply chain participants, ensuring security and transparency.

2. Internet of Things (IoT): Enables real-time tracking of products and conditions throughout the supply chain.
3. Artificial Intelligence (AI): Analyzes vast amounts of supply chain data to identify patterns and predict potential issues.

4. RFID and QR codes: Provide unique identifiers for products, enabling precise tracking and tracing.
Several companies have successfully implemented transparent and traceable supply chains. For example, Patagonia uses traceability to ensure that its wool suppliers adhere to animal welfare standards, promoting ethical practices across the supply chain. De Beers, the world's largest diamond producer, uses blockchain to track diamonds from the mine to the final consumer, ensuring that the diamonds are conflict-free and ethically sourced.

Case Studies in Ethical Supply Chains
Several businesses have successfully implemented fair trade practices and ethical supply chains, demonstrating that it is possible to balance profitability with social and environmental responsibility.

1. Ahimsa Footwear: Ahimsa, the world's first 100% vegan

footwear factory, embodies fair and sustainable trade principles in its operations. The company ensures decent wages, good working conditions, and gender equality. With 40 employees producing 200 pairs of shoes daily, Ahimsa has proven that it's possible to create quality products without animal exploitation while maintaining ethical labor practices.

2. Provenance and Subway: These companies have leveraged blockchain technology to achieve traceability and authenticity in their supply chains. This implementation has enhanced trust and operational efficiency.

3. Ajinomoto: The food and biotech company has implemented transparent supply chain strategies to reduce its environmental impact. By switching packaging materials, Ajinomoto reduced virgin plastic use by about 2,000 tonnes annually for its Blendy coffee products.

4. Braskem: The company invested $290 million in a renewable polyethylene plant and implemented a Responsible Ethanol Sourcing Framework. These initiatives demonstrate Braskem's commitment to sustainable and transparent supply chains.

5. AGCO: The agricultural equipment manufacturer introduced a global Transport Management System (TMS) that cut freight costs by 18% in 18 months while improving environmental sustainability.

Improving corporate ethics and sustainability requires a number of measures, including bringing the ahimsa concept into international commerce, guaranteeing fair salaries and working conditions, and making supply chains more transparent and traceable. The case studies show that corporations may be profitable while still being socially and environmentally responsible.

Businesses must drastically alter their operations and decision-making processes to accommodate these ideas. It necessitates thinking for the future with an eye on the welfare of all parties involved, including communities, the environment, and employees. Despite the difficulty, this strategy has several advantages, such as a better reputation for the business, more efficient operations, and more trust from consumers.

Supply chains will become more transparent and traceable as a result of ongoing innovation in technologies such as the internet of things (IoT) and blockchain. In order to tackle complicated issues and establish more fair and long-lasting global trade systems, it is crucial that corporations, governments, and civil society groups continue to work together.

By incorporating these ideas and practices into their operations and connections with all stakeholders, businesses may help create a more equitable and sustainable global economy.

References

1. Times of India. (2024, September 30). Embracing Ahimsa. Retrieved from https://timesofindia.indiatimes.com/speaking-tree/daily-ecstasy/embracing-ahimsa/articleshow/113798926.cms
2. Sustainability Magazine. (2024, November 20). Top 10: Ethical Labour Practices in Supply Chains. Retrieved from https://sustainabilitymag.com/top10/top-10-ethical-labour-practices-in-supply-chains
3. Propel Apps. (n.d.). Supply Chain Traceability: The Ultimate Guide. Retrieved from https://propelapps.com/blog/mobile-supply-chain/supply-chain-traceability/
4. Ahimsa. (n.d.). Our inspirers and defenders of the animal cause. Retrieved from https://en.useahimsa.com/we-are-ahimsa
5. Venuez.dk. (n.d.). Successful Implementation of Transparent Supply Chains. Retrieved from https://www.venuez.dk/case-studies-successful-implementation-of-transparent-supply-chains/
6. UNESCO. (n.d.). Ahmisa (Non-Violence), Gandhi and Global Citizenship Education (GCED). Retrieved from https://www.unesco.org/en/articles/ahmisa-non-violence-gandhi-and-global-citizenship-education-gced

Chapter 10: Mindful Marketing and Advertising

In an era of information overload and increasing consumer skepticism, mindful marketing and advertising have emerged as crucial approaches for businesses seeking to build trust, foster loyalty, and create lasting value. This chapter explores the principles of truthful communication in marketing, the promotion of conscious consumption, and the application of ethical persuasion techniques.

Truthful Communication in Marketing

Mindful advertising and marketing rests on the bedrock of truthful communication. Since information travels at the speed of light in today's linked world and customers have unparalleled access to evaluations and corporate details, being truthful is not only the right thing to do, but also essential for success in business.

The value of honest advertising cannot be emphasized enough. "Dishonesty may backfire" when it comes to advertising, says Content Garden. In today's fast-paced world of rapid communication and social media, deceitful advertising may swiftly cause a reaction from consumers and harm to a company's image. In its place, firms should "communicate honestly, authentically and transparently" in order to gain consumers' confidence and foster long-term partnerships.

Key principles of truthful communication in marketing include:
1. Accuracy in product descriptions: Providing clear, accurate, and comprehensive information about products and services is essential. This includes being upfront about both the strengths and limitations of offerings.
2. Transparency in pricing and policies: Clearly disclosing all costs, fees, and terms of service helps build trust and prevents

misunderstandings that could lead to customer dissatisfaction.
3. Honesty about company practices: Being open about business operations, sourcing, and production methods can differentiate a brand and appeal to consumers who value transparency.
4. Authenticity in brand messaging: Ensuring that marketing messages align with the company's actual values and practices is crucial for maintaining credibility.
5. Open communication about mistakes: When errors occur, acknowledging them openly and explaining how they will be addressed can strengthen customer relationships.

The benefits of truthful communication extend beyond avoiding negative consequences. As noted by Content Garden, "Honest content creates trust" and can be a powerful tool for customer retention and loyalty. By providing accurate and valuable information, businesses can position themselves as trusted advisors in their respective fields.

Implementing truthful communication in marketing requires a commitment from all levels of an organization. It involves:

1. Establishing clear guidelines for marketing communications
2. Training employees on the importance of honesty and transparency
3. Implementing review processes to ensure accuracy in all marketing materials
4. Encouraging a culture of openness and accountability

Promoting Conscious Consumption

As consumers become increasingly aware of the environmental and social impacts of their purchasing decisions, promoting conscious consumption has become a key aspect of mindful marketing. Conscious consumption involves making purchasing decisions based not only on personal needs and desires but also on the broader implications of those choices for society and the environment.

The rise of conscious consumerism is driven by several factors:

1. Increased awareness of environmental issues
2. Growing concern about social justice and labor practices
3. Desire for healthier and more sustainable lifestyles
4. Access to information about product sourcing and production methods

For businesses, promoting conscious consumption can align with both ethical principles and strategic goals. As noted in the article from KoltiTrace Shop, key elements of conscious consumption include "the use of sustainable materials, ethical sourcing and production, reduced waste, fair labor practices, and support for local and independent businesses".

Strategies for promoting conscious consumption through marketing include:

1. Educating consumers: Providing information about the environmental and social impacts of products can help consumers make more informed choices.

2. Highlighting sustainable features: Emphasizing eco-friendly materials, ethical production methods, or fair labor practices can appeal to conscious consumers.

3. Encouraging responsible use: Marketing messages that promote product longevity, repair, and recycling can support more sustainable consumption patterns.

4. Transparency in supply chains: Providing information about product origins and production methods can build trust and appeal to consumers seeking ethical options.

5. Supporting causes: Aligning with environmental or social causes can demonstrate a commitment to conscious business practices.

The benefits of promoting conscious consumption extend beyond appealing to a growing market segment. It can also:

1. Enhance brand reputation and loyalty
2. Drive innovation in product design and production methods
3. Attract and retain employees who value ethical business practices
4. Contribute to long-term business sustainability

However, it's crucial that efforts to promote conscious consumption are genuine and backed by real action. As the article from 2 Stallions points out, "56% of consumers today believe that many companies use environmental and social responsibility as a marketing ploy to generate profits". To avoid being perceived as engaging in "greenwashing", businesses must ensure that their marketing messages align with their actual practices and commitments.

Ethical Persuasion Techniques

Ethical persuasion in marketing involves influencing consumer behavior through honest, transparent, and responsible practices. Unlike manipulative tactics that may deceive or exploit, ethical persuasion respects consumer autonomy and fosters trust through integrity and openness.

Brian Ahearn, as cited by Paul Andrew Smith, defines ethical persuasion based on three criteria:

1. It is good for the person you're influencing, not just good for you.
2. It contains honest communication, and nothing important is left out.
3. It uses psychology that's natural and appropriate for the situation.

Ahearn outlines seven principles of ethical persuasion:

1. Reciprocity: Giving something of value and trusting you'll receive in return.
2. Liking: Building genuine connections with customers.

3. Authority: Demonstrating expertise in your field.
4. Consensus: Providing social proof that others are choosing your product or service.
5. Consistency: Aligning actions with words and commitments.
6. Scarcity: Highlighting legitimate limitations in availability.
7. Unity: Emphasizing shared experiences and identities.

Implementing these principles in marketing requires careful consideration and a commitment to ethical practices. For example, while scarcity can be a powerful motivator, it's only ethical if the scarcity is genuine and not artificially created to pressure consumers.

Ethical persuasion techniques can be applied across various marketing channels:

1. Content Marketing: Creating valuable, informative content that addresses customer needs and concerns.

2. Social Media: Engaging in honest, transparent communication and fostering genuine connections with followers.

3. Email Marketing: Respecting subscriber preferences and providing clear opt-out options.

4. Advertising: Ensuring all claims are truthful and substantiated, and avoiding misleading visuals or language.

5. Sales Processes: Training sales teams to prioritize customer needs and provide honest product information.

The benefits of ethical persuasion in marketing are numerous. As noted by Atomic Social, they include:

1. Enhanced Consumer Trust: Transparency in marketing helps build consumer trust, leading to increased loyalty.

2. Increased Brand Credibility: Brands consistently engaging in ethical practices are viewed as more credible and reliable.

3. Long-term Customer Relationships: Ethical persuasion is key to developing enduring relationships with customers.

4. Reduced Legal and Ethical Risks: Transparent marketing practices minimize the risk of legal issues related to deceptive advertising.

Mindful marketing and advertising, characterized by truthful communication, promotion of conscious consumption, and the use of ethical persuasion techniques, offer a path forward for businesses seeking to build lasting relationships with consumers in an increasingly complex and scrutinized marketplace.

By prioritizing honesty, transparency, and ethical considerations in their marketing efforts, businesses can not only avoid the pitfalls of deceptive practices but also differentiate themselves in a crowded market, build strong brand loyalty, and contribute to positive societal and environmental outcomes.

As consumers become more discerning and demand greater accountability from the brands they support, the principles of mindful marketing are likely to become not just ethical imperatives but essential strategies for business success and sustainability in the 21st century.

References
1. Atomic Social. (n.d.). The Art of Ethical Persuasion: Building Trust and Loyalty with Transparent Marketing Practices. Retrieved from https://atomicsocial.com/the-art-of-ethical-persuasion-building-trust-and-loyalty-with-transparent-marketing-practices/
2. Content Garden. (n.d.). Why honesty in marketing is the best approach. Retrieved from https://content-garden.com/why-honesty-in-marketing-is-the-best-approach
3. KoltiTrace Shop. (n.d.). The Rise of Conscious

Consumption: Understanding the Importance of Sustainable Living. Retrieved from https://www.koltiva.com/post/the-rise-of-conscious-consumption-understanding-the-importance-of-sustainable-living

4. Smith, P. A. (n.d.). 7 Principles of Ethical Persuasion. LinkedIn. Retrieved from https://www.linkedin.com/pulse/7-principles-ethical-persuasion-paul-andrew-smith

5. Stallions. (2024, April 25). The Rise of the Conscious Consumer: How Sustainability Became a Market Force. Retrieved from https://2stallions.com/blog/the-rise-of-the-conscious-consumer-how-sustainability-became-a-market-force/

Chapter 11: Ethical Banking and Finance

Ethical banking and finance have gained increasing attention in recent years as consumers and institutions seek financial practices aligned with moral and religious principles. This chapter explores ethical finance through a dharmic lens, examining perspectives on interest and usury, the role of microfinance in promoting financial inclusion, and parallels between Islamic banking principles and dharmic concepts.

Interest and Usury in Dharmic Perspective

Many ethical and religious traditions, especially dharmic religions, have disagreed on the practice of lending money with interest. Despite interest-based lending's centrality to modern financial systems, several religious writings and academics have long criticized it as exploitative.

Excessive interest or usury was vehemently denounced in Hindu texts. The ancient Hindu law scripture known as the Manusmriti states: "Behave like Shudras to the cowboys, traders, cooks, dancers, slaves and to the Brahmins who devour usury." Because of this, members of the highest caste, the Brahmins, should be shunned if they engage in usury. The Brihod Dharma Purana is another Hindu scripture that says, "Do not take the food of the physicians, beggars, usurers, atheists, and rogues." These verses show how ancient Hindu culture felt about usury.

The Buddhist religion likewise frowned upon usury. A dishonest existence, according to the Buddha, includes dealing with usury, lying, betrayal, and deception. Doing good deeds and not hurting other people are important tenets of Buddhism, thus this makes sense.

Be that as it may, these traditions did not condemn interest per such, but rather usury in particular. People from many walks of life and eras have argued about where to draw the line between legitimate interest and usury.

A number of contemporary academics have argued for a more complex understanding of dharmic traditions. When it benefits society and the economy as a whole, they imply that modest, non-exploitative interest could be OK. This view is consistent with the dharmic notion of meditating on conflicting viewpoints and adjusting one's code of ethics accordingly.

Similar arguments about interest and usury occur in Abrahamic religions as well as dharmic traditions. The morality of loans with interest has long been a point of contention among the Abrahamic faiths. The fundamental principle of Islamic banking is the Islamic prohibition of riba, which is commonly translated as interest or usury.

This universal worry about the morality of interest-bearing loans is reflective of a deeper human sense of equity and non-exploitation in monetary dealings. Ethical financial systems, according to the paper, need to weigh the interest's function and the good and bad effects it might have on society.

Microfinance and Financial Inclusion

Microfinance has emerged as a powerful tool for promoting financial inclusion and alleviating poverty, aligning closely with dharmic principles of compassion and social responsibility. By providing small loans and other financial services to underserved populations, microfinance institutions aim to empower individuals and communities to improve their economic circumstances.

The concept of microfinance aligns with several dharmic principles:

1. Compassion and service: Microfinance seeks to help those in need, reflecting the dharmic emphasis on seva (selfless service) and karuna (compassion).

2. Self-reliance: By providing tools for economic empowerment rather than handouts, microfinance supports the dharmic value of self-effort and personal responsibility.

3. Interconnectedness: Microfinance recognizes the ripple effects of individual economic empowerment on families and communities, reflecting the dharmic understanding of interconnectedness.

4. Ethical wealth creation: Microfinance aims to create wealth in an ethical manner, supporting legitimate economic activities rather than exploitative practices.

Microfinance has had a major effect in expanding access to banking services. Microfinance has helped more than 6.2 crore individual borrowers in India, with 12 crore accounts in total, according to latest statistics. Over 14.2 million families have benefited from microfinance thanks to the SHG-Bank Linkage Programme run by the National Bank for Agriculture and Rural Development (NABARD). This initiative has been made possible by 119 million SHGs.

When it comes to empowering women, microfinance has made a huge difference. Among women, 51% are now aware of microcredit loans, and 11% have actually taken out one, according to the 2019–2020 National Family Health Survey (NFHS). Women are able to have greater financial independence and influence in household financial decisions as a result of this expansion of financial services.

Micro, small, and medium-sized enterprises (MSMEs) run by women may also gain from microfinance's expansion. In India, women run about 13.5–15.7 million businesses, with more than 95% of those being micro-enterprises. Microfinance has a substantial potential to address the Rs. 836 billion unmet loan demand for women-owned very small businesses (WVSEs), according to a research from the International Finance Corporation (IFC) in 2022.

On the other hand, microfinance does have its share of problems. Some people are worried about aggressive collection techniques, excessive interest rates, and being overly indebted. In order for microfinance to fulfill its promise of empowering and including people, these problems show how important it is to regulate it carefully and implement ethical principles.

Microfinance practices are in harmony with the dharmic view of artha, or material wealth, as a tool, not an objective in and of itself. Microfinance views financial services as a way to empower individuals and communities to better their lives, similar to how dharmic traditions regard wealth as a tool for completing one's obligations and responsibilities.

Islamic Banking Principles and Their Dharmic Parallels

Islamic banking, based on the principles of Sharia law, offers an alternative model of finance that shares several parallels with dharmic ethical concepts. While arising from different religious traditions, Islamic finance and dharmic approaches to ethics in finance often arrive at similar conclusions about ethical economic practices.

Key principles of Islamic banking include:

1. Prohibition of riba (interest): Islamic finance prohibits the charging or paying of interest, considering it a form of exploitation. This aligns with the dharmic critiques of usury discussed earlier.

2. Risk-sharing: Islamic finance emphasizes the sharing of profit and loss between financial institutions and their clients. This principle reflects the dharmic concept of karma, where actions and their consequences are intrinsically linked.

3. Asset-backing: Islamic financial transactions must be backed by tangible assets, avoiding purely speculative activities. This principle aligns with the dharmic emphasis on creating real value rather than engaging in deceptive or harmful economic practices.

4. Ethical investments: Islamic finance prohibits investments in activities considered haram (forbidden), such as alcohol production or gambling. This parallels dharmic concepts of ethical livelihood and avoiding harmful activities.

5. Social responsibility: Many Islamic financial institutions emphasize social responsibility and community development, reflecting the dharmic principle of seva (selfless service).

These principles of Islamic finance find numerous parallels in dharmic ethical concepts:

1. Prohibition of exploitation: Both Islamic and dharmic traditions emphasize fairness in economic transactions and condemn exploitation. The Islamic prohibition on riba aligns with dharmic critiques of usury.

2. Emphasis on real economic activity: Islamic finance's focus on asset-backed transactions and prohibition of speculative activities aligns with dharmic emphasis on creating genuine value through one's work.

3. Ethical investment: The Islamic concept of avoiding haram investments parallels dharmic principles of ethical livelihood and avoiding harmful activities.

4. Social responsibility: Both traditions emphasize the importance of using wealth for the greater good of society, reflecting shared values of compassion and community service.

5. Holistic view of economics: Both Islamic finance and dharmic traditions view economic activities as part of a broader ethical and spiritual framework, rather than as purely material

pursuits.

An expanded, cross-cultural comprehension of ethical finance may be possible in light of the similarities between Islamic banking and dharmic ethical principles. The particular regulations and procedures may vary, but the fundamental moral considerations frequently coincide, indicating the presence of common human principles in commercial endeavors.

Islamic banking and dharmic financial ethics both have obstacles when tried to be applied to contemporary economic systems. Some people think that Islamic financial products could be in violation of Sharia rules as they are just advanced versions of interest-based goods that are common in the West. Equally complex is the process of interpreting and adapting ancient dharmic ethical concepts for use in contemporary financial markets.

Conventional financial systems put profit first, but ethical banking and finance, seen through a dharmic perspective, provide a strong alternative. A more complete system of finance that takes into account material requirements as well as moral and religious concerns can be imagined by looking at microfinance's function in expanding access to banking services, similarities between Islamic banking principles and dharmic ideas, and different viewpoints on interest and usury.

From a dharmic point of view, we should not think of money in a vacuum, but rather as a thread in a larger tapestry of moral obligations and personal development. It urges us to think about how our economic decisions will affect our communities and the environment in the long run, not only in the short term.

The concepts of ethical finance covered in this chapter provide useful information for developing more fair and sustainable economic systems at a time when we are confronting increasing global problems including social fragmentation, environmental degradation, and inequality. We may strive for an economy that does more than just make money; by incorporating these ethical ideals into our financial processes, we can help people thrive and develop spiritually.

References

1. Mahmood, M. (n.d.). Prohibition of Riba is not only a Muslim thing! LinkedIn. https://www.linkedin.com/pulse/prohibition-riba-only-muslim-thing-mabroor-mahmood
2. Corporate Finance Institute. (n.d.). Islamic Banking - Understanding Its Principles, Origin, Tools, and Challenges. https://corporatefinanceinstitute.com/resources/career-map/sell-side/capital-markets/islamic-finance/
3. Investopedia. (n.d.). Islamic Banking and Finance Definition: History and Example. https://www.investopedia.com/terms/i/islamicbanking.asp
4. Protium. (n.d.). 4 ways microfinance is promoting financial inclusion in India. https://protium.co.in/microfinance-role-in-india/

Chapter 12: Socially Responsible Investing

Socially responsible investing (SRI) has gained significant traction in recent years as investors increasingly seek to align their financial decisions with their values and ethical principles. This chapter explores SRI through a dharmic lens, examining how Environmental, Social, and Governance (ESG) criteria align with dharmic principles, the relationship between impact investing and dharma, and methods for measuring social and environmental returns on investments.

ESG Criteria Through a Dharmic Lens

Environmental, Social, and Governance (ESG) criteria provide a framework for assessing an organization's business practices and performance on various sustainability and ethical issues. When viewed through a dharmic lens, these criteria take on additional depth and significance, aligning closely with principles of interconnectedness, non-violence, and ethical conduct central to dharmic traditions.

Environmental Criteria:

The environmental component of ESG aligns closely with the dharmic principle of ahimsa (non-violence) extended to the natural world. Key environmental factors in ESG include:

1. Climate change mitigation
2. Energy efficiency
3. Water management
4. Pollution control
5. Waste and resource management
6. Deforestation prevention
7. Biodiversity protection

These factors reflect a holistic approach to environmental

stewardship that resonates with dharmic concepts of interconnectedness and responsibility towards nature. For example, the emphasis on biodiversity protection aligns with the Jain principle of respecting all forms of life, while efforts to combat climate change reflect the dharmic understanding of the interconnectedness of all beings and the need for balance in natural systems.

Social Criteria:
The social component of ESG encompasses a company's relationships with various stakeholders, including employees, customers, suppliers, and local communities. Key social factors include:
1. Human rights observance
2. Compliance with labor standards
3. Customer satisfaction measures
4. Data protection and privacy safeguards
5. Promotion of gender equality and diversity
6. Employee engagement strategies
7. Community relations initiatives

These criteria align closely with dharmic principles of social responsibility and ethical conduct. The emphasis on human rights and fair labor practices reflects the dharmic concept of dharma as duty or righteous living. The focus on diversity and community relations aligns with the principle of vasudhaiva kutumbakam (the world is one family), encouraging businesses to consider their broader social impact.

Governance Criteria: Governance factors in ESG focus on the internal systems of control and oversight within an organization. Key governance factors include:
1. Executive pay
2. Board composition and diversity
3. Anti-bribery and corruption measures
4. Lobbying regulations
5. Oversight of political contributions

6. Implementation of whistleblower schemes

These criteria align with dharmic principles of ethical leadership and transparency. The emphasis on fair compensation and diverse representation in leadership reflects the dharmic ideal of balanced and inclusive decision-making. Anti-corruption measures and whistleblower protections align with the dharmic emphasis on satya (truthfulness) in all dealings.

Impact Investing and Its Alignment with Dharma

Impact investing, which aims to generate positive social and environmental impacts alongside financial returns, aligns closely with dharmic principles of ethical wealth creation and social responsibility. The core tenets of impact investing resonate with several key dharmic concepts:

1. Interconnectedness: Impact investing recognizes the interconnected nature of social, environmental, and economic systems, reflecting the dharmic understanding of the world as an interconnected whole.

2. Ahimsa (non-violence): By directing capital towards solutions that address social and environmental challenges, impact investing seeks to minimize harm and promote positive outcomes, aligning with the principle of ahimsa.

3. Karma: The concept of karma, which emphasizes the consequences of one's actions, is reflected in impact investing's focus on the long-term effects of investment decisions.

4. Dharma (duty): Impact investing can be seen as a way of fulfilling one's dharma or duty to society and the environment through responsible allocation of financial resources.

5. Aparigraha (non-possession): While impact investing does not reject wealth creation, it aligns with the principle of aparigraha by emphasizing the use of wealth for broader societal

benefit rather than mere accumulation.

The alignment between impact investing and dharmic principles is evident in the criteria used to evaluate impact investments. According to research, impact investments must meet three key criteria:
1. Intend to generate societal impact alongside financial returns
2. Create a change that would not have occurred otherwise
3. Make a difference that is appropriately assessed and tracked

These criteria reflect the dharmic emphasis on intentionality, positive change, and accountability in one's actions.

Measuring Social and Environmental Returns

Measuring the social and environmental returns of investments is crucial for ensuring the effectiveness and credibility of socially responsible investing practices. Several methodologies have been developed to quantify these non-financial returns, many of which align with dharmic principles of holistic assessment and long-term thinking.

Social Return on Investment (SROI): SROI is a method for measuring values that are not traditionally reflected in financial statements, including social, economic, and environmental factors. The SROI process typically includes the following steps:

1. Identify stakeholders
2. Map results
3. Assign value to results
4. SROI calculation
5. Communicate results

This approach aligns with the dharmic principle of considering the broader impact of one's actions on all stakeholders. The SROI calculation is expressed as a ratio, where a 2:1 ratio indicates that $2 of social value is created from a $1 investment.

Impact Measurement and Management (IMM): IMM is a more

comprehensive approach that integrates impact considerations throughout the investment lifecycle. The elea Foundation's Impact Measurement Methodology (eIMM) is an example of this approach, quantifying expected impact in "elea Impact Points" that allow comparison across various business models, sectors, and geographies.

This methodology aligns with the dharmic emphasis on holistic assessment and continuous improvement. By integrating impact measurement across the investment process, it reflects the dharmic principle of mindfulness in all actions.

Environmental, Social, and Governance (ESG) Metrics: ESG metrics provide a framework for assessing the sustainability and ethical impact of investments. While specific metrics vary, they typically cover areas such as carbon emissions, labor practices, and board diversity. These metrics align with dharmic principles by providing a comprehensive view of an organization's impact beyond financial performance.

Challenges and Considerations:
Measuring social and environmental returns presents several challenges:

1. Quantifying intangible benefits: Many social and environmental impacts are difficult to express in monetary terms.
2. Attribution: Determining the extent to which observed changes are due to a specific investment can be complex.
3. Long-term effects: Some impacts may only become apparent over extended periods, requiring long-term monitoring.
4. Standardization: The lack of universally accepted standards for impact measurement can make comparisons difficult.

These challenges reflect the complexity of assessing dharmic principles in practice, where the full consequences of actions may not be immediately apparent and require nuanced consideration.

From a dharmic perspective, socially responsible investment provides a robust framework for bringing one's financial choices into harmony with one's moral and spiritual values. Investors may build portfolios that do good for society and the environment while still making money by combining environmental, social, and governance (ESG) criteria with impact investing strategies and strong assessment procedures.

Since SRI methods are congruent with dharmic ideals, they may be useful instruments for bringing dharmic ethics into the contemporary financial sphere. A more sustainable, egalitarian, and spiritually aligned economic system may be achieved by combining dharmic knowledge with modern investing strategies, which is particularly relevant in light of the increasing global issues we are facing.

References

1. Content Garden. (n.d.). Why honesty in marketing is the best approach. Retrieved from https://content-garden.com/why-honesty-in-marketing-is-the-best-approach
2. Corporate Finance Institute. (n.d.). Islamic Banking - Understanding Its Principles, Origin, Tools, and Challenges. https://corporatefinanceinstitute.com/resources/career-map/sell-side/capital-markets/islamic-finance/
3. elea. (n.d.). The importance of impact measurement in impact investing. Retrieved from https://www.elea.org/en/blog/post/the-importance-of-impact-measurement-in-impact-investing
4. Greenly. (2022, September 29). ESG criteria: what you need to know. Retrieved from https://greenly.earth/en-us/blog/company-guide/esg-criteria-what-you-need-to-know
5. Harvard Business Review. (2020, November 30). Calculating the Value of Impact Investing. Retrieved from https://hbr.org/2019/01/calculating-the-

value-of-impact-investing
6. HBS Online. (n.d.). What Is Impact Measurement? Retrieved from https://online.hbs.edu/blog/post/what-is-impact-measurement
7. Investopedia. (n.d.). What Factors Go Into Calculating Social Return on Investment (SROI)? Retrieved from https://www.investopedia.com/ask/answers/070314/what-factors-go-calculating-social-return-investment-sroi.asp
8. Oxford Centre for Hindu Studies. (n.d.). OCHS and Dow Jones. Retrieved from https://ochs.org.uk/ochs-and-dow-jones/
9. Pew Research Center. (2021). Jainism: One of the world's oldest religions. Retrieved from [URL not provided]
10. TechTarget. (2024, October 9). What is ESG (Environmental, Social and Governance)? Retrieved from https://www.techtarget.com/whatis/definition/environmental-social-and-governance-ESG

Chapter 13: Alternative Currencies and Local Economies

In recent years, there has been a lot of buzz about alternative currencies and local economic systems. This is because communities are looking for methods to make their economies stronger, build social connections, and make their models more robust and sustainable. Economic localization, time banking, and talent exchanges are the three main tenets of this movement that are examined in this chapter.

Complementary Currency Systems

An alternate exchange medium that complements national currencies in order to accomplish social, environmental, or economic objectives is called a complementary currency system. These systems are designed to supplement existing conventional currencies by tackling specific community or regional issues, not to supplant them.

"Any currency or exchange medium that is not a national currency but is accepted for use under specific conditions in a nation" is defined as a "complementary currency" in Investopedia (n.d.). Usually, private individuals, advocacy organizations, or official regulatory agencies issue these currencies to cater to particular needs or regions.

Key characteristics of complementary currencies include:

1. Limited scope: They are often designed for use within a specific region or for particular types of transactions.
2. Social or environmental goals: Many complementary currencies aim to achieve objectives such as promoting local spending, encouraging sustainable practices, or fostering community connections.
3. Parallel operation: They function alongside national

currencies rather than replacing them entirely.
4. Diverse forms: Complementary currencies can take various forms, from physical notes to digital credits or even time-based systems.

Among the many examples of complementary currencies, the Berkshire area of Massachusetts's usage of BerkShares stands out. More than 300 establishments have begun taking BerkShares as payment, demonstrating the success of the initiative to promote local spending and investment (Investopedia, n.d.). Community currencies are those that have as their stated purpose the promotion of regional or local economic development.

The idea of carbon credits is another intriguing illustration. Although cap-and-trade systems for controlling carbon emissions are not commonly thought of as currencies, they work in a manner similar to complementary currencies. An industry-specific market has emerged for the purchase and sale of carbon credits, which allow businesses to lawfully release carbon (Investopedia, n.d.).

One interesting method for dealing with supplementary currencies is the Japanese Fureai Kippu system. When people volunteer their time to assist the elderly, they accumulate electronic credits that may be used for future care or shared with others. This technique has been adopted by other Asian nations dealing with comparable demographic difficulties since it was first implemented in 1995 in Japan (Investopedia, n.d.).

Complementary currencies can offer several benefits:

1. Localized economic stimulus: By encouraging spending within a specific region, these currencies can help keep wealth circulating locally.
2. Social cohesion: Many complementary currencies foster community connections and mutual support networks.
3. Environmental sustainability: Some systems are designed to

incentivize eco-friendly practices or support local, sustainable businesses.

4. Financial inclusion: Complementary currencies can provide access to economic activities for individuals who may be marginalized in the traditional financial system.

However, these systems also face challenges, including limited acceptance, potential for volatility or inflation (depending on the issuing process), and regulatory complexities.

Time Banking and Skill Exchanges

A supplementary monetary system, time banking employs time itself as a unit of exchange. Members of a time bank accrue credits by helping others, which they may then redeem for further services. Regardless of the service kind, this method treats everyone's time equally.

"Time Banks are community initiatives which enable people to exchange goods and services using time as money," reads an assessment of the Broadway Skills Exchange Time Bank. According to York (n.d.), this is structured as an exchange of services. This method provides a fresh perspective on how to acknowledge and reward efforts that conventional economic frameworks may fail to do so.

Key features of time banking include:

1. Equal valuation of time: One hour of service is typically worth one time credit, regardless of the skill level or type of service provided.
2. Reciprocity: Participants both give and receive services, fostering a sense of mutual support and community engagement.
3. Skill diversity: Time banks often encompass a wide range of skills and services, from practical tasks to professional expertise.
4. Social inclusion: By valuing all contributions equally, time

banks can provide opportunities for participation to individuals who may be marginalized in the traditional job market.

The Broadway Skills Exchange Time Bank, which focused on homeless individuals, demonstrated several positive outcomes:
1. Increased engagement: The time bank successfully engaged many homeless individuals who were distant from formal work and learning opportunities.
2. Enhanced self-worth: Participants reported a greater sense of dignity and self-worth through the recognition of their skills and time.
3. Tangible benefits: The ability to exchange time credits for education, training, or other services was highly valued by participants.
4. Pathway to employment: Some participants used time banking as a stepping stone to self-employment or formal employment opportunities.

The evaluation reported that over two years, 50 people secured employment as a direct result of time banking, and another 23 entered accredited external training (York, n.d.).

Skill exchanges, which often operate on similar principles to time banks, provide platforms for individuals to trade their expertise or abilities directly with others in their community. These systems can help build local resilience by fostering a diverse skill base within a community and encouraging mutual support networks.

Strengthening Local Communities through Economic Localization

Economic localization refers to the process of shifting economic activities and resources towards local communities, promoting self-reliance, sustainability, and resilience. This approach aligns closely with the principles behind complementary currencies and time banking, emphasizing the importance of local relationships and community-based economic activities.

According to FasterCapital, economic localization offers several benefits for local economies:

1. Strengthening local businesses: By prioritizing local purchases, consumers create increased demand for local goods and services, leading to job creation and economic growth within the community.
2. Retaining wealth: When money is spent locally, it circulates within the community, creating a multiplier effect that benefits multiple local businesses and individuals.
3. Fostering resilience and self-sufficiency: Reducing dependency on external sources for essential goods and services can make communities less vulnerable to disruptions in global supply chains.
4. Promoting sustainability: Local production and consumption often result in reduced transportation needs and more sustainable resource use.
5. Preserving cultural diversity: Supporting local businesses and traditions can help maintain the unique character and cultural heritage of a community.
6. Building stronger communities: Face-to-face interactions and support for local initiatives can foster stronger social bonds and a sense of collective responsibility (FasterCapital, n.d.).

By establishing a medium of exchange unique to a certain area or group of people, community currencies are an essential component in economic localization. As a result, reliance on foreign markets is diminished, and domestic commerce and consumption are fostered. For instance, according to FasterCapital (n.d.), the Bristol Pound in the UK has effectively boosted economic resilience by encouraging locals to patronize local firms.

When it comes to localizing economic activity, the idea of "community wealth building" provides a holistic perspective. Working with local government institutions and other "anchor institutions" like hospitals and educational institutions is where this strategy starts, according to Neva Goodwin. These groups may utilize their purchasing power to back locally owned, socially conscious companies as they care about the community and have no plans to leave (Goodwin, 2023).

The Cleveland Model, with its model cooperatives like Evergreen, shows how this strategy may work. The Cleveland Clinic, Case Western Reserve University, and University Hospitals are three nonprofits that have recently begun purchasing critical services from local vendors, creating an opportunity for worker-owned companies in the area. This change maintained monetary circulation, opened doors to decent employment, and enriched the society as a whole (Goodwin, 2023).

To build stronger, more sustainable, and more socially linked communities, there are potent instruments at our disposal, such as alternative currencies, time banking, and economic localization. Innovative initiatives like these can supplement conventional economic systems, allowing communities to better meet their unique requirements, foster a sense of mutual support, and open up economic possibilities to all.

These neighborhood-based economic models could gain traction as problems like global warming, income disparity, and social isolation gain steam. They provide solutions to strengthen the economy, bring people together, and make consumption and manufacturing more sustainable.

Regulatory roadblocks, low acceptability, and the necessity for continuous community involvement and education are some of the difficulties that can arise from putting these systems into action. More study and testing is needed to perfect these models' execution and make the most of their beneficial effects on local economies and communities as they spread and change.

References

1. FasterCapital. (n.d.). Economic Localization: Empowering Local Economies with CC. Retrieved from https://fastercapital.com/content/Economic-Localization--Empowering-Local-Economies-with-CC.html
2. Goodwin, N. (2023). Going Local: Strengthening Local Economies by Building from the Bottom Up. Boston University. Retrieved from https://www.bu.edu/eci/2023/04/10/going-local-strengthening-local-economies-by-building-from-the-bottom-up/
3. Investopedia. (n.d.). Complementary Currency: What It Is, How It Works, and Examples. Retrieved from https://www.investopedia.com/terms/c/complementary-currency-cc.asp
4. York. (n.d.). An Evaluation of the Broadway Skills Exchange Time Bank. Retrieved from https://www.york.ac.uk/media/chp/documents/2014/Broadway%20Time%20Bank%20Final%20Report%201%20May%202014.pdf

Chapter 14: Philanthropy and Dana (Giving)

There are profound lessons for contemporary philanthropy and CSR in the ancient practice of dana (giving), which has its origins in dharmic traditions. Discussing how corporate giving programs might connect with dharmic principles, this chapter investigates the principle of dana in dharmic contexts and looks at techniques for enhancing philanthropic effect.

The Concept of Dana in Dharmic Traditions

Hinduism, Sikhism, Buddhism, Jainism, and Dana (meaning "giving" or "gift" in Sanskrit and Pali) are central to the dharmic traditions. It includes contributing to charity, serving others without expecting anything in return, and other types of selfless giving.

Dana is frequently mentioned as the first of the ten paramitas (perfections) that a bodhisattva must develop, and it is widely believed to be one of the most significant spiritual practices in Buddhism. One way to develop knowledge, compassion, and non-attachment is to practice dana. In the Oxford Bibliographies it is stated that "Dana can refer variously to alms to monastics, royal largesse, patronage to temples, gifts of ritual payment for services, hospitality to the stranger, and charity to the poor and needy".

The motivations and effects of dana are subjects of extensive discussion in Buddhist texts. Some key points of debate include:
1. The relative merit of giving to different recipients (e.g., monastics vs. the poor)
2. The appropriate mindset and motivation for giving
3. The karmic effects of different types of gifts

4. The relationship between the giver and recipient

Dana is an important practice for spiritual development and social responsibility fulfillment in Hinduism, and it is strongly related to the idea of dharma (duty or righteousness). The ancient Hindu law document known as the Manusmriti punishes those who indulge in excessive profit-seeking or usury and stresses the significance of dana.

Dana is highly valued in Jainism as well, especially for its role in sustaining the monastic community and sharing religious wisdom. One Jain literature defines dana as "a term signifying a gift or act of charity; often associated with religious offerings" in the Trishashti Shalaka Purusha Caritra.

Giving and receiving dana is considered as a spiritual exercise that helps all parties involved in dharmic traditions, rather than merely a monetary transaction. It is said to foster qualities like empathy, objectivity, and connection.

Strategic Philanthropy for Maximum Impact

While the concept of dana in dharmic traditions emphasizes the spiritual benefits of giving, modern approaches to philanthropy often focus on maximizing the tangible impact of charitable contributions. Strategic philanthropy aims to align philanthropic efforts with clearly defined goals and measurable outcomes.

Key principles of strategic philanthropy include:

1. Defining a clear purpose: As noted by Lisa Alston, CSR executive, "Start by defining a clear purpose for your philanthropic initiatives. Ask yourself what social or environmental issues align with your company's values and mission"[3].
2. Setting measurable goals: Establish clear, measurable goals for philanthropic efforts and use key performance indicators (KPIs) to track progress and impact.

3. Collaboration: Partner with other organizations, both within and outside your industry, to amplify the impact of philanthropic initiatives.
4. Long-term commitment: Think beyond one-time donations and commit to long-term partnerships with nonprofits for sustained impact.
5. Leveraging skills and expertise: Offer more than just financial support by sharing your company's skills and expertise to help nonprofits operate more efficiently.
6. Transparency and reporting: Communicate philanthropic efforts transparently and share progress reports with stakeholders to build trust.

Research by Exponent Philanthropy identified several factors that drive philanthropic impact:
1. Focused grantmaking: Foundations with highly focused grantmaking reported higher levels of impact compared to those with unfocused strategies.
2. Incorporating racial equity: Foundations that considered racial equity highly relevant to their mission tended to report higher levels of impact.
3. Providing long-term, flexible funding: Sustained efforts over time, supported by flexible funding, can help foundations and grantees achieve their goals more effectively.
4. Going beyond the grant: Leveraging a foundation's position and reputation to convene stakeholders and foster collaboration can amplify impact.
5. Soliciting feedback: Collecting and acting on feedback from grantees and community members provides valuable insights for continuous improvement.

By implementing these strategies, philanthropic organizations can increase their effectiveness and create more significant, lasting change in their focus areas.

Corporate Giving Programs Aligned with Dharmic Values

Corporate giving programs offer an opportunity for businesses to contribute to society while potentially enhancing their reputation and employee engagement. When aligned with dharmic values, these programs can create meaningful impact while fostering a sense of purpose and interconnectedness within the organization.

Key elements of corporate giving programs that align with dharmic values include:

1. Emphasis on selfless service: Encourage employee volunteering and create opportunities for staff to engage in acts of service without expectation of personal gain.
2. Focus on addressing root causes: Align giving programs with efforts to address systemic issues rather than just treating symptoms, reflecting the dharmic emphasis on understanding the interconnected nature of social problems.
3. Holistic approach: Consider the broader impact of giving programs on all stakeholders, including employees, communities, and the environment.
4. Long-term commitment: Develop sustained partnerships with nonprofit organizations, reflecting the dharmic view of dana as an ongoing spiritual practice rather than a one-time transaction.
5. Transparency and ethical conduct: Ensure that giving programs are implemented with integrity and transparency, aligning with dharmic principles of truthfulness and ethical behavior.

Several companies have implemented giving programs that exemplify these principles:

Google's Employee Giving Program: Employees can earn awards for their service hours and participate in a matching gift program. This method enhances the effect of workers' efforts while also encouraging them to practice dana on an individual level.

Environmental Action by Patagonia: As part of its 1% for the Planet effort, Patagonia has pledged to donate one percent of their sales to environmental organizations. Responsible stewardship and interconnection are dharmic values, and this dedication to environmental stewardship over the long term is in line with them.

A Program by The Coca-Cola Company: 5by20 Through the provision of financial services, business skill training, and other tools, this worldwide project seeks to empower five million female entrepreneurs. Dharmic principles of emancipation and getting to the heart of societal problems are reflected in the program.

Microsoft's Employee Giving Program: With the help of matching gifts and volunteer opportunities, Microsoft encourages its workers to give back to their communities. This campaign exemplifies the dharmic idea of community responsibility for social welfare by raising millions of dollars for different charity groups.

When implementing corporate giving programs aligned with dharmic values, companies should consider the following:
1. Authenticity: Ensure that giving programs genuinely reflect the company's values and are not merely public relations exercises.
2. Employee engagement: Involve employees in shaping and implementing giving programs to foster a sense of ownership and purpose.
3. Measurable impact: Develop clear metrics to assess the impact of giving programs and communicate results transparently.
4. Continuous learning: Regularly review and refine giving programs based on feedback and outcomes, reflecting the dharmic emphasis on self-reflection and growth.
5. Holistic integration: Align giving programs with broader corporate social responsibility initiatives and business practices

to create a coherent approach to social impact.

Charity and corporate giving in the current day might draw philosophical wisdom from the dharmic traditions' idea of dana. Giving programs may be designed to optimize effect while simultaneously fostering a culture of generosity, connection, and social responsibility by merging the spiritual and ethical components of dana with strategic philanthropy methods.

Wisdom from dharmic traditions may help companies and nonprofits handle the complicated problems of the 21st century. Organizations may foster a feeling of purpose and fulfillment among their stakeholders while also contributing to a more compassionate, egalitarian, and sustainable society by connecting their donation programs with dharmic ideals.

A robust foundation for making good change that lasts is provided by combining dana principles with contemporary charitable techniques. In order to create more efficient, moral, and spiritually congruent methods of giving and social impact, it is crucial that we keep investigating how modern practices interact with traditional wisdom.

References

1. Investopedia. (n.d.). Complementary Currency: What It Is, How It Works, and Examples. Retrieved from https://www.investopedia.com/terms/c/complementary-currency-cc.asp
2. York. (n.d.). An Evaluation of the Broadway Skills Exchange Time Bank. Retrieved from https://www.york.ac.uk/media/chp/documents/2014/Broadway%20Time%20Bank%20Final%20Report%201%20May%202014.pdf
3. Alston, L. (n.d.). Strategic Philanthropy: Guiding Principles for Maximizing CSR Impact. LinkedIn. Retrieved from https://www.linkedin.com/pulse/strategic-philanthropy-guiding-principles-maximizing-csr-lisa-alston-cfude
4. McCormick, B. (n.d.). Philanthropic

Impact: Key Strategies and Factors. Exponent Philanthropy. Retrieved from https://exponentphilanthropy.org/blog/philanthropic-impact-key-strategies-and-factors/
5. 360MatchPro. (2024, September 19). 15 Inspiring Examples of Corporate Philanthropy in Action. Retrieved from https://360matchpro.com/corporate-philanthropy-examples/
6. Wisdom Library. (2024, October 24). Dana, Dāna, Daṅa: 48 definitions. Retrieved from https://www.wisdomlib.org/definition/dana
7. Ramana Maharshi Organization. (n.d.). Dharma in the Workplace Hinduism and Business Ethics. Retrieved from https://www.ramana-maharshi.org/dharma-in-the-workplace-hinduism-and-business-ethics/
8. Oxford Bibliographies. (n.d.). Buddhism - Dāna. Retrieved from https://www.oxfordbibliographies.com/display/document/obo-9780195393521/obo-9780195393521-0215.xml
9. Finance Strategists. (n.d.). Corporate Giving Programs | Meaning, Types, Pros, & Cons. Retrieved from https://www.financestrategists.com/wealth-management/corporate-social-responsibility-csr/corporate-giving-programs/

Chapter 15: Wealth Distribution and Economic Equality

Concerns about economic inequality and the distribution of wealth have recently emerged as major themes in discussions about the world economy. In this chapter, we will look at income redistribution and progressive taxes from a dharmic viewpoint, as well as the idea of universal basic income, and how dharmic values might guide our efforts to alleviate economic disparity.

Addressing Income Inequality Through Dharmic Principles

Social tensions and economic instability have been exacerbated by the enormous growth in income disparity in several nations over the past few decades. When it comes to finding a long-term, ethical solution to this problem, dharmic traditions have a lot to teach.

Dharma is a moral code that encourages doing the right thing and being responsible members of society. In the context of equitable distribution of wealth, this idea promotes the responsible and altruistic use of money by the well-off for the benefit of everyone. The ancient Hindu law document known as the Manusmriti states that the affluent have an obligation to contribute financially to religious organizations, carry out rites of sacrifice, and help those in need.

Under the dharmic principle of interconnectedness, which is articulated in ideas like "Vasudhaiva Kutumbakam" or "the world is one family"), severe economic disparity is detrimental to both the economically disadvantaged and society at large. This is in line with current economic research that has shown that extreme inequality can hinder social mobility and economic progress.

Key dharmic principles that can inform approaches to addressing income inequality include:

1. Dana (giving): The practice of charitable giving is highly valued in dharmic traditions. Encouraging voluntary redistribution of wealth through philanthropy can help address inequality while fostering a sense of social responsibility among the wealthy.

2. Aparigraha (non-possession): This principle, particularly emphasized in Jainism, encourages minimizing material possessions and avoiding excessive accumulation of wealth. Applied to modern economics, it suggests policies that discourage extreme concentration of wealth.

3. Karma (action and its consequences): The concept of karma encourages individuals to consider the long-term consequences of their economic actions, both for themselves and for society. This can promote more ethical and sustainable business practices.

4. Dharma (duty/righteousness): The idea that individuals have duties based on their social position suggests that those with greater wealth and power have a corresponding responsibility to use their resources for the greater good.

5. Ahimsa (non-violence): While typically associated with physical non-violence, ahimsa can be extended to economic relationships, encouraging business practices and policies that do not exploit or harm others.

Implementing these principles in modern economic policy could involve:

1. Encouraging corporate social responsibility initiatives aligned with dharmic values
2. Developing tax incentives for charitable giving and socially responsible investing
3. Promoting education and awareness about the societal impacts of extreme inequality
4. Supporting fair labor practices and living wages

5. Investing in public goods and services that benefit all members of society

Progressive Taxation and Wealth Redistribution

Progressive taxation, where tax rates increase as income or wealth increases, is a key tool for addressing economic inequality. When viewed through a dharmic lens, progressive taxation can be seen as a formalized system for fulfilling the duty of the wealthy to contribute more to society.

The concept of progressive taxation aligns with several dharmic principles:

1. Proportional responsibility: The idea that those with greater resources have a greater responsibility to contribute to society's well-being.

2. Interconnectedness: Recognizing that individual prosperity is interconnected with societal well-being, justifying higher contributions from those who have benefited most from the social and economic system.

3. Moderation: Discouraging excessive accumulation of wealth by increasing the tax burden at higher income levels.

The World Inequality Report 2022 highlights the potential of progressive wealth taxes to generate significant revenue for addressing societal challenges. The report suggests that modest progressive taxes on global multimillionaires could generate up to 1.6% of global incomes, which could be reinvested in education, health, and environmental initiatives.

Implementing progressive taxation from a dharmic perspective might involve:

1. Designing tax brackets that reflect dharmic principles of proportional responsibility
2. Earmarking tax revenues from the highest brackets for initiatives that benefit the broader community

3. Incorporating non-financial forms of contribution (e.g., community service) into the tax system
4. Developing transparency mechanisms to show how tax revenues are used for societal benefit

However, it's important to note that excessive taxation could potentially conflict with dharmic principles if it discourages productive economic activity or infringes on individual liberty. The goal should be to find a balance that promotes social welfare while still incentivizing innovation and entrepreneurship.

Wealth redistribution through taxation should be complemented by other measures to address root causes of inequality, such as:
1. Investing in education and skill development to enhance economic opportunities
2. Implementing policies to prevent rent-seeking and unethical wealth accumulation
3. Supporting small businesses and entrepreneurship to broaden wealth creation
4. Strengthening social safety nets to prevent extreme poverty

Universal Basic Income from a Dharmic Perspective

Universal Basic Income (UBI) is a policy proposal that would provide all citizens with a regular, unconditional sum of money to cover basic needs. When examined through a dharmic lens, UBI presents both opportunities and challenges.

Alignment with Dharmic Principles:

1. Universality: The universal nature of UBI aligns with the dharmic concept of the inherent dignity and value of all individuals.
2. Reducing suffering: By providing a basic level of economic security, UBI could help alleviate poverty and reduce suffering, aligning with the dharmic emphasis on compassion.
3. Enabling self-realization: With basic needs met, individuals

may have more opportunity to pursue spiritual and personal growth, a key aspect of dharmic traditions.

4. Recognizing interconnectedness: UBI acknowledges the shared stake all members of society have in the economy, reflecting dharmic ideas of interconnectedness.

Challenges from a Dharmic Perspective:

1. Work ethic: Some interpretations of dharma emphasize the importance of work and fulfilling one's duties. There may be concerns that UBI could discourage productive activity.
2. Moral hazard: The unconditional nature of UBI might be seen as conflicting with the dharmic emphasis on karma and personal responsibility.
3. Resource allocation: Ensuring that a UBI system doesn't divert resources from other important social needs would be crucial from a dharmic perspective.

The Indian government's Economic Survey 2016-17 explored the concept of UBI through a uniquely Indian lens, including considerations of dharmic principles. The survey noted that UBI could promote many basic values of a society that respects all individuals as free and equal, aligning with dharmic ideals of human dignity.

However, the survey also highlighted potential conflicts with dharmic thought, referencing a quote attributed to Mahatma Gandhi expressing concern about providing free meals to those who haven't worked for them. This reflects the tension between unconditional support and the dharmic emphasis on duty and effort.

Implementing UBI in a manner consistent with dharmic principles might involve:

1. Coupling UBI with opportunities for community service or personal development
2. Designing the system to complement rather than replace

existing social support structures

3. Emphasizing UBI as a tool for enabling individuals to better fulfill their dharma, rather than as an end in itself

4. Incorporating elements of reciprocity or conditionality that align with dharmic values while maintaining the core universality of the program

Dharmic principles provide a fresh viewpoint on economic equality and income distribution by bringing together material, ethical, and spiritual issues. We can create strategies for progressive taxes, wealth redistribution, and UBI that foster economic equity and personal development by referencing ideas like dana, karma, and dharma.

Everyone, including the rich, suffers when there is severe inequality, as the dharmic focus on interconnections serves as a reminder. Meanwhile, everyone, regardless of their financial situation, is encouraged to give their utmost because of the emphasis on personal responsibility and obligation.

A more sustainable, fair, and satisfying economic system might be created by combining dharmic wisdom with current economic policy, which could be helpful as we face increasing economic inequities and the social implications they bring. Wealth, according to this perspective, should not be seen as a goal in and of itself but rather as a tool to improve people's lives and the world at large.

To improve these ideas and create real policies that successfully combine economic efficiency with dharmic ethical ideals, further study and testing are required. We may strive towards economic systems that provide riches while simultaneously encouraging spiritual development and societal peace if we keep investigating how ancient knowledge intersects with modern economic problems.

References

1. Adikka Channels. (n.d.). Ethical Principles Of Wealth Management In Sanatana Dharma. https://adikkachannels.com/ethical-principles-of-wealth-management-in-sanatana-dharma/
2. World Inequality Lab. (2022). World Inequality Report 2022. https://wir2022.wid.world/chapter-7/
3. Government of India. (2017). Economic Survey 2016-17. https://www.indiabudget.gov.in/budget2017-2018/es2016-17/echap09.pdf
4. Bourguignon, F. (2018). Spreading the Wealth. Finance & Development, 55(1). https://www.imf.org/en/Publications/fandd/issues/2018/03/bourguignon
5. FaithInvest. (n.d.). What one of the world's oldest religions says about investing. https://www.faithinvest.org/post/what-one-of-the-world-s-oldest-religions-says-about-investing
6. Investopedia. (2024). What Is a Progressive Tax? Advantages and Disadvantages. https://www.investopedia.com/terms/p/progressivetax.asp
7. Oxford Bibliographies. (n.d.). Buddhism - Dāna. https://www.oxfordbibliographies.com/display/document/obo-9780195393521/obo-9780195393521-0215.xml
8. Wisdom Library. (2024). Dana, Dāna, Daṅa: 48 definitions. https://www.wisdomlib.org/definition/dana

Chapter 16: The Concept of Swadharma in Career Choices

The ancient concept of swadharma, or one's own duty, offers valuable insights for navigating career choices in the modern economy. This chapter explores how individuals can find their true calling, align their work with personal values and skills, and approach the gig economy and freelancing through a dharmic lens.

Finding One's True Calling in the Modern Economy

The significance of finding and achieving one's individual life's purpose or calling is highlighted by the idea of swadharma. Finding a line of work that fits one's personality, abilities, and life circumstances is an important part of making a career decision. "You can find your swadharma by reflecting on what you love to do," Chinmaya Udghosh said. What kind of employment engrosses you the most? What is it that you are good at and find easy to do?

Given the abundance of work opportunities and frequent job changes that people encounter in today's market, this journey of self-discovery is more important than ever. According to the Bhagavad Gita, which is a sacred text, swadharma is paramount.

The 'obligation' of another person who has done their job properly is better than one's own 'duty,' even if it lacks substance. "It is better to die doing one's own duty than to do the duty of another, which is full of fear and produces positive danger."

Rather of striving for perfection in a job that doesn't fit one's character, this poem says that it's preferable to follow one's genuine calling, flaws and all. This notion, when applied to contemporary career pathways, stresses the importance of doing meaningful work rather than chasing after traditionally successful but ultimately unsatisfying jobs.

To discover one's swadharma in the modern economy, individuals can:
1. Reflect on their natural inclinations and passions
2. Identify skills that come easily to them
3. Consider the impact they want to make in the world
4. Explore various career options through internships or informational interviews
5. Seek guidance from mentors or career counselors

It's important to note that finding one's true calling is often an ongoing process rather than a one-time discovery. As individuals grow and evolve, their understanding of their swadharma may also shift.

Aligning Work with Personal Values and Skills

Finding a career path that fits one's values and abilities is the next step after discovering one's swadharma. Achieving happiness and professional success in the long run requires this harmony.

Ethical behavior and making a positive impact on society via one's profession are central to the dharmic view. "Dharma can mean 'duty,' 'goodness,' or 'doing the right thing,' and it tells us how people and society should behave according to Hindu beliefs," observes the article on dharma in the workplace. It's a beacon that everyone in the office, from upper management on down, can follow to make ethical decisions while keeping the greater good and integrity of the company in mind.

To align work with personal values and skills, individuals can:
1. Identify core values: Reflect on what principles are most important in life and work.
2. Assess skills and strengths: Conduct a thorough inventory of natural abilities, acquired skills, and areas of expertise.

3. Research industries and roles: Explore career options that allow for the expression of personal values and utilization of key skills.
4. Seek purpose-driven organizations: Look for companies or organizations whose missions align with personal values.
5. Create opportunities: If existing roles don't fully align, consider entrepreneurship or intrapreneurship to create a position that better fits one's swadharma.
6. Continuous learning: Invest in developing skills that support both personal growth and career advancement in alignment with one's values.

The process of aligning work with personal values and skills may involve making difficult choices, such as turning down lucrative opportunities that don't align with one's swadharma. However, the dharmic perspective suggests that such choices ultimately lead to greater fulfillment and positive impact.

The Gig Economy and Freelancing Through a Dharmic Lens

The rise of the gig economy and freelancing has created new opportunities and challenges for individuals seeking to align their work with their swadharma. From a dharmic perspective, these flexible work arrangements can be seen as both an opportunity for greater self-expression and a potential source of instability.

The gig economy, characterized by short-term contracts and freelance work, has grown significantly in recent years. According to a report cited by iPleaders, "By 2030, the Niti Aayog anticipates a 200 percent increase in gig jobs." This trend offers individuals more flexibility in choosing work that aligns with their skills and values.

From a dharmic perspective, the gig economy can be viewed through several lenses:
1. Flexibility and autonomy: The ability to choose projects and clients can allow individuals to better align their work with

their swadharma.

2. Ethical considerations: Freelancers have the opportunity to be selective about the projects they take on, potentially avoiding work that conflicts with their values.

3. Uncertainty and instability: The lack of job security in the gig economy may conflict with the dharmic emphasis on fulfilling one's duties and responsibilities.

4. Continuous learning: The need to adapt and acquire new skills in the gig economy aligns with the dharmic principle of personal growth and self-improvement.

5. Work-life balance: Flexible work arrangements can support a more holistic approach to life, allowing time for spiritual practices and personal development.

When approaching the gig economy through a dharmic lens, individuals should consider:

1. Intention and purpose: Reflect on whether freelancing or gig work aligns with one's broader life purpose and values.

2. Ethical client selection: Choose clients and projects that align with personal values and contribute positively to society.

3. Balancing flexibility and stability: While embracing the freedom of gig work, also consider ways to create financial stability and security.

4. Continuous skill development: Invest in learning and growth to stay relevant and valuable in the gig economy.

5. Building meaningful relationships: Despite the transient nature of gig work, strive to create genuine connections with clients and colleagues.

6. Maintaining work-life harmony: Use the flexibility of gig work to create a balanced lifestyle that supports both professional and personal growth.

Freelancing and the gig economy provide amazing chances for people to live out their swadharma, but it's important to think things through and make deliberate decisions so that they don't conflict with dharmic values.

If you're trying to figure out what to do with your life after college, the idea of swadharma can serve as a helpful guide. Finding one's life's job, making sure it fits in with one's beliefs and abilities, and being attentive when dealing with new forms of employment like the gig economy are all ways that the dharmic worldview may help people lead more satisfying and meaningful lives at work.

People should keep in mind that discovering and practicing their swadharma is a lifelong effort as they strive to incorporate these principles into their professional lives. To succeed, one must be introspective, flexible, and prepared to make decisions that run counter to popular opinion. But people might discover more purpose and fulfillment in their jobs if they are themselves and have a positive impact on the world via what they do.

A person can find clarity, purpose, and integrity in navigating the difficulties of professional choices by drawing on the timeless knowledge of dharmic principles, which can be a guiding light in the fast changing modern economic world.

References

1. Chinmaya Udghosh. (n.d.). Aligning with Swadharma: Walking the Talk in Your Career. Retrieved from https://www.chinmayaudghosh.in/career/aligning-with-swadharma-walking-the-talk-in-your-career
2. iPleaders. (n.d.). All about freelancing and gig economy. Retrieved from https://blog.ipleaders.in/all-about-freelancing-and-gig-economy/
3. Muskoka Yoga Festival. (n.d.). Svadharma (One's Own Duty) - Yoga Philosophy Glossary. Retrieved from https://muskokayogafestival.com/yoga-philosophy-glossary/svadharma-ones-own-duty/
4. Paramporulfoundation. (n.d.). How can finding your Svadharma lead to a better life? Retrieved from https://www.paramporulfoundation.com/how-can-

finding-your-svadharma-lead-to-a-better-life/
5. Ramana Maharshi Organization. (n.d.). Dharma in the Workplace Hinduism and Business Ethics. Retrieved from https://www.ramana-maharshi.org/dharma-in-the-workplace-hinduism-and-business-ethics/
6. Scroll.in. (n.d.). This book asks if the Hindu philosophy of dharma and swadharma can make for better workplace leaders. Retrieved from https://scroll.in/article/1071339/this-book-asks-if-the-hindu-philosophy-of-dharma-and-swadharma-can-make-for-better-workplace-leaders
7. Unbroken Self. (n.d.). Svadharma, Values and Balancing Work and Inquiry. Retrieved from https://www.unbrokenself.com/svadharma-values-and-balancing-work-and-inquiry/

Chapter 17: Workplace Spirituality and Well-being

Integrating spirituality and wellness practices is becoming more vital for firms and individuals in today's fast-paced and demanding work environment. Creating caring and growth-oriented work settings, seeing work-life balance as a spiritual practice, and integrating meditation and mindfulness in the workplace are the three main themes that this chapter focuses on to investigate the notions of workplace spirituality and well-being.

Integrating Meditation and Mindfulness in the Workplace

In recent years, there has been a surge in the popularity of mindfulness and meditation programs in the workplace. Many companies have come to realize the many benefits these programs can have on employee health and performance. One effective strategy for improving health and output on the job is mindfulness training, which is paying undivided attention in the here and now without attaching any value judgments to what one observes.

Reducing stress levels is one of the main advantages of practicing mindfulness at work. Research shows that mindfulness training in the workplace may significantly improve well-being, decrease perceived stress, and decrease burnout. The idea behind the practice is to live in the now and not dwell on the past or the future. Improved mental health and a sense of peace can result from decreased levels of cortisol, the stress hormone (Shift Workspaces, n.d.).

Implementing mindfulness practices in the workplace can take various forms:

1. Short mindful exercises: Alidina (2018) suggests using short

mindful exercises throughout the workday. These can be as brief as a few minutes and can be easily incorporated into busy schedules.
2. Mindful reminders: Setting reminders to practice mindfulness can help employees avoid slipping into "auto-pilot" mode. For example, associating phone notifications with a moment of mindfulness can serve as a regular prompt for conscious awareness (Alidina, 2018).
3. Mindfulness training programs: Organizations can offer structured mindfulness training programs to employees, providing them with tools and techniques to incorporate mindfulness into their daily work routines.
4. Mindful meetings: Incorporating mindfulness into meetings by starting with a brief meditation or moment of silence can help participants focus and engage more effectively.

The benefits of integrating mindfulness in the workplace extend beyond stress reduction. Research has shown that mindfulness practices can lead to:

1. Enhanced focus and concentration: Mindfulness exercises help employees cultivate greater focus and concentration, enabling them to work more efficiently and with increased attention to detail (Shift Workspaces, n.d.).
2. Improved emotional regulation: Mindfulness equips individuals with tools to manage their emotions effectively, particularly in high-stress situations. This leads to healthier interactions and decision-making processes (Persona, n.d.).
3. Increased resilience: The practice of mindfulness builds resilience, empowering employees to handle workplace challenges with grace and flexibility (Persona, n.d.).
4. Enhanced creativity and innovation: A calm and focused mind fostered by mindfulness practices can lead to increased creativity and innovative thinking (Shift Workspaces, n.d.).
5. Better decision-making: Mindfulness encourages a non-reactive and non-judgmental mindset, enabling individuals to

approach challenges and decisions with clarity and objectivity (Shift Workspaces, n.d.).

By incorporating these practices, organizations can create a more balanced, productive, and harmonious work environment that supports both individual and collective well-being.

Work-life Balance as a Spiritual Practice

Achieving a healthy work-life balance is not just about managing time effectively; it can also be viewed as a spiritual practice that contributes to overall well-being and personal growth. The concept of work-life balance aligns closely with spiritual principles such as mindfulness, presence, and holistic living.

Work-life balance is important because it reduces stress, helps avoid burnout, increases job satisfaction, and improves overall health and well-being (Persona, 2024). When approached as a spiritual practice, work-life balance can lead to a deeper sense of purpose, fulfillment, and connection to oneself and others.

Key aspects of viewing work-life balance as a spiritual practice include:
1. Being present in the moment: As emphasized by Attorney With a Life (n.d.), being present is a crucial spiritual practice that can be applied to both work and personal life. This involves focusing fully on the task at hand, whether it's a work project or spending time with family and friends.
2. Cultivating gratitude: Practicing gratitude for both work accomplishments and personal experiences can help foster a positive mindset and increase overall life satisfaction (Attorney With a Life, n.d.).
3. Recognizing the temporary nature of challenges: Understanding that difficult work situations or personal issues are temporary can help maintain perspective and reduce stress (Attorney With a Life, n.d.).
4. Aligning work with personal values: Ensuring that one's work

aligns with personal values and contributes to a greater purpose can bring a sense of spiritual fulfillment to professional life.
5. Practicing self-care: Prioritizing self-care activities such as exercise, meditation, and hobbies is essential for maintaining spiritual and emotional well-being.

Implementing work-life balance as a spiritual practice can lead to numerous benefits, including:
1. Improved physical and mental health: A balanced lifestyle is essential for maintaining good physical and mental health, reducing the risk of chronic health conditions and promoting overall well-being (Persona, 2024).
2. Increased productivity: By effectively managing work and personal time, individuals can approach their work with greater enthusiasm, creativity, and motivation, leading to increased productivity (Persona, 2024).
3. Enhanced relationships: Prioritizing personal relationships and social connections outside of work can lead to stronger support networks and improved overall life satisfaction (Corporate Wellness Magazine, n.d.).
4. Greater sense of purpose: Aligning work and personal life with one's values and spiritual beliefs can lead to a deeper sense of purpose and fulfillment.
5. Reduced burnout: Maintaining a healthy work-life balance can prevent feelings of being overwhelmed and significantly reduce the risk of burnout (Persona, n.d.).

Organizations can support employees in achieving work-life balance as a spiritual practice by:
1. Offering flexible work arrangements
2. Encouraging the use of vacation time and personal days
3. Providing resources for stress management and personal development
4. Fostering a culture that values work-life balance and personal well-being

By viewing work-life balance as a spiritual practice, individuals and organizations can create a more holistic and fulfilling approach to both professional and personal life.

Creating Nurturing and Growth-Oriented Work Environments

Developing a nurturing and growth-oriented work environment is essential for promoting workplace spirituality and well-being. Such environments foster personal and professional growth, encourage creativity and innovation, and contribute to overall employee satisfaction and engagement.

Key elements of creating a nurturing and growth-oriented work environment include:
1. Establishing core values: Laying out clear core values that reflect the organization's commitment to employee well-being and growth can provide a foundation for a positive workplace culture (Built In, 2024).
2. Promoting diversity and inclusivity: Creating an inclusive work culture that welcomes individuals from all backgrounds and celebrates their differences is crucial for fostering a nurturing environment (Built In, 2024).
3. Encouraging idea-sharing: Empowering all employees to share their ideas, regardless of their position in the company, can lead to innovation and a sense of value among team members (Built In, 2024).
4. Implementing employee recognition programs: Recognizing and rewarding employees for their achievements can motivate them to continue performing at high levels and feel valued within the company (Built In, 2024).
5. Providing growth opportunities: Offering professional development programs, mentorship opportunities, and clear career progression paths can support employee growth and engagement.
6. Fostering open communication: Promoting transparency and open communication between all levels of the organization can create a culture of trust and collaboration (Built In, 2024).
7. Shifting perspectives on mistakes and failure: In a growth-

oriented organization, mistakes and failures are viewed as opportunities for learning and improvement rather than reasons for punishment (Spearity, 2023).

8. Treating employees as whole persons: Recognizing employees as individuals with lives outside of work and showing interest in their personal well-being can foster a more nurturing work environment (Spearity, 2023).

The benefits of creating a nurturing and growth-oriented work environment are numerous:
1. Increased employee engagement and satisfaction
2. Higher retention rates and reduced turnover
3. Enhanced creativity and innovation
4. Improved overall organizational performance
5. Stronger employer brand and ability to attract top talent

By implementing these strategies, organizations can create work environments that not only support employee well-being but also contribute to the overall success and growth of the business.

References
1. Attorney With a Life. (n.d.). Work-Life Balance—the spiritual side. Retrieved from https://www.attorneywithalife.com/work-life-balance-the-spiritual-side/
2. Built In. (2024). Work Culture: 12 Ways to Create a Positive Environment. Retrieved from https://builtin.com/company-culture/positive-work-culture
3. Corporate Wellness Magazine. (n.d.). The Importance of Work-Life Balance for Employee Well-Being. Retrieved from https://www.corporatewellnessmagazine.com/article/the-importance-of-work-life-balance-for-employee-well-being
4. Persona. (2024). Benefits Of Mindfulness In The Workplace.

5. Persona. (2024). Work-Life Balance: Why It's Important And How To Achieve It. Retrieved from https://www.personatalent.com/productivity/how-to-achieve-work-life-balance/
6. Shift Workspaces. (n.d.). The Benefits of Mindfulness in the Workplace. Retrieved from https://shiftworkspaces.com/the-benefits-of-mindfulness-in-the-workplace/
7. Spearity. (2023). Creating a Growth-Oriented Culture in Your Organization. Retrieved from https://www.spearity.com/2023/04/25/creating-a-growth-oriented-culture-in-your-organization/

Chapter 18: Fair Labor Practices and Workers' Rights

The application of dharmic principles to labor laws, ethical treatment of workers, and alternative business models like worker cooperatives offers a compelling framework for creating more just and sustainable labor practices. This chapter explores how dharmic concepts can inform labor regulations, examines approaches to ethical employee treatment, and presents case studies of successful worker-owned cooperatives.

Applying Dharmic Principles to Labor Laws

Labor laws play a crucial role in protecting workers' rights and ensuring fair treatment in the workplace. When viewed through a dharmic lens, these laws take on additional ethical significance and can be seen as a means of upholding fundamental principles of justice, compassion, and human dignity.

Key dharmic principles that can inform labor laws include:
1. Dharma (duty/righteousness): The concept of dharma emphasizes fulfilling one's duties and responsibilities. In the context of labor laws, this principle can be applied to both employers and employees, encouraging mutual respect and fair treatment.
2. Ahimsa (non-violence): While typically associated with physical non-violence, ahimsa can be extended to economic relationships, promoting workplace safety and preventing exploitation.
3. Satya (truthfulness): This principle can inform regulations around transparent hiring practices, clear communication of job expectations, and honest financial reporting.
4. Aparigraha (non-possessiveness): Applied to labor laws, this principle could encourage fair distribution of profits and

discourage excessive accumulation of wealth at the expense of workers.

5. Karma (action and its consequences): This concept can inform regulations that hold employers accountable for their actions and decisions that affect workers.

The application of these principles to labor laws can be seen in several key areas:

1. Fair Wages: The principle of dharma suggests that employers have a duty to provide fair compensation for work performed. This aligns with modern concepts of minimum wage laws and equal pay for equal work.

2. Safe Working Conditions: Ahimsa (non-violence) applied to the workplace emphasizes the importance of ensuring worker safety and health. This principle supports regulations mandating safe working environments, proper safety equipment, and health protections.

3. Non-Discrimination: The dharmic emphasis on the inherent dignity of all beings aligns with laws prohibiting workplace discrimination based on factors such as race, gender, religion, or age.

4. Work-Life Balance: Dharmic principles emphasize the importance of balance in all aspects of life. This can inform regulations around maximum working hours, mandatory rest periods, and paid time off.

5. Collective Bargaining Rights: The dharmic concept of sangha (community) supports workers' rights to organize and collectively negotiate with employers.

As noted in the iPleaders article, Indian labor laws are founded on principles of social justice, social equity, and social security (iPleaders, n.d.). These principles align closely with dharmic concepts and aim to create a more equitable and just work environment.

Ethical Treatment of Employees and Contractors

Ethical treatment of employees and contractors goes beyond mere compliance with labor laws and involves creating a workplace culture that values and respects all workers. From a dharmic perspective, this approach recognizes the interconnectedness of all beings and the importance of fostering positive relationships in all aspects of life, including work.

Key aspects of ethical employee treatment include:
1. Fair Compensation: Providing wages and benefits that allow workers to meet their basic needs and support their families.
2. Respect and Dignity: Treating all workers with respect, regardless of their position or status within the organization.
3. Professional Development: Offering opportunities for skill development and career advancement.
4. Work-Life Balance: Respecting employees' personal time and family commitments.

5. Transparent Communication: Maintaining open and honest communication about company policies, expectations, and performance.
6. Inclusive Decision-Making: Involving employees in decision-making processes that affect their work and well-being.
7. Ethical Supply Chain Management: Ensuring that contractors and suppliers also adhere to ethical labor practices.

Implementing these principles can lead to numerous benefits for both employees and organizations. As noted in the article by Shift Workspaces, ethical treatment of employees can result in increased productivity, improved employee retention, enhanced company reputation, and ultimately, better business outcomes (Shift Workspaces, n.d.).

For contractors and gig workers, ethical treatment involves additional considerations:
1. Fair Contracts: Providing clear, equitable contracts that outline expectations, compensation, and terms of engagement.

2. Timely Payment: Ensuring prompt payment for services rendered.
3. Reasonable Deadlines: Setting realistic timelines for project completion.
4. Professional Development: Offering opportunities for skill enhancement, even for temporary workers.
5. Integration: Treating contractors as valued team members, even if they are not permanent employees.

Case Studies of Worker-Owned Cooperatives

Worker-owned cooperatives represent an alternative business model that aligns closely with dharmic principles of equity, shared responsibility, and collective well-being. These organizations are owned and democratically controlled by their workers, offering a unique approach to labor relations and business management.

Several case studies illustrate the potential of worker cooperatives:

1. Uralungal Labour Contract Cooperative Society Limited (ULCCS Ltd): This Indian construction cooperative, founded in 1925, has over 2,000 workers, including 750 members engaged in construction work. ULCCS Ltd emphasizes professional governance, from policy formulation to financial management. Key features include:
- Democratic decision-making: Only workers can be elected as directors, and each director is assigned responsibility for project execution.
- Fair wages: Workers receive daily wages higher than market rates, along with additional benefits like provident funds.
- Continuous learning: Members attend cooperative education and training programs.
- Empowerment: Workers are free to make appropriate decisions within prescribed procedures, fostering leadership skills.

The success of ULCCS Ltd demonstrates how worker cooperatives can combine democratic principles with professional management to create a thriving, ethical business (ijirem, n.d.).

2. Mondragon Corporation: Based in the Basque region of Spain, Mondragon is one of the world's largest worker cooperatives. It comprises multiple cooperatives across various industries and has significant economic impact. Key lessons from Mondragon include:
- Comprehensive training: Mondragon emphasizes ongoing, multi-dimensional training in democratic work processes and technical skills.
- Educational infrastructure: The corporation has established specialized centers, a polytechnic school, a university, and a global entrepreneurship program.
- Social security: Mondragon has developed its own social security system for workers.

Mondragon's success demonstrates how worker cooperatives can scale while maintaining democratic principles and prioritizing worker well-being (HR Magazine, n.d.).

3. Namasté Solar: This U.S.-based solar energy installer offers insights into financial transparency and collaborative growth:
- Open-book management: Owner-members have access to company financials and participate in regular discussions of important data and decisions.
- Scaling through collaboration: After expanding to other states, Namasté Solar encouraged the formation of similar cooperatives in a collaborative network.

Namasté Solar's approach shows how transparency and collaboration can support robust worker participation and sustainable growth (HR Magazine, n.d.).

4. CECOSESOLA (Central de las Cooperativas de Lara): This

Venezuelan cooperative group, with about 20,000 consumer and worker members across dozens of affiliated cooperatives, is known for its unique communication practices:
- Continuous open-ended communications: Regular conversations cover workplace issues, values, and serve as venues for conflict resolution and community building.
- CECOSESOLA's model demonstrates how open communication can foster a strong cooperative culture and address workplace challenges effectively (HR Magazine, n.d.).

5. Earthworker Cooperative: This Australian second-tier cooperative coordinates member cooperatives like Earthworker Energy Manufacturing Cooperative. Key features include:
- Cross-border collaboration: Earthworker collaborates with Argentine worker-recuperated enterprises to create similar cooperatives.
- Integration of social movements: The cooperative embodies an ethic of worker self-organization, bridging labor and environmental activism.

Earthworker's approach shows how worker cooperatives can address broader social and environmental concerns while providing ethical employment (HR Magazine, n.d.).

These case studies illustrate several key benefits of worker cooperatives:

1. Democratic control: Workers have a say in decision-making processes that affect their work and livelihoods.
2. Equitable profit-sharing: Profits are distributed more fairly among workers rather than being concentrated at the top.
3. Job security: Worker-owners are less likely to lay themselves off during economic downturns.
4. Community investment: Cooperatives often prioritize local community development and environmental sustainability.
5. Skills development: Many cooperatives emphasize ongoing training and education for their members.

However, worker cooperatives also face challenges, including:

1. Access to capital: Traditional financial institutions may be hesitant to lend to cooperatives.
2. Complexity in decision-making: Democratic processes can sometimes slow down decision-making.
3. Balancing social goals with market pressures: Cooperatives must navigate competing priorities of worker well-being and business competitiveness.
4. Lack of awareness: Many people are unfamiliar with the cooperative model, which can make it difficult to attract customers or new members.

Despite these challenges, worker cooperatives offer a promising model for aligning business practices with dharmic principles of equity, shared responsibility, and collective well-being.

References

1. HR Magazine. (n.d.). Collaboration in action: Success stories of cooperative business. Retrieved from https://www.hrmagazine.co.uk/content/comment/collaboration-in-action-success-stories-of-cooperative-business/
2. ijirem. (n.d.). Labour Laws: Concept, Origin, Objectives and Classification. Retrieved from https://ijirem.org/DOC/4-labour-laws-concept-origin-objectives.pdf
3. iPleaders. (n.d.). Labour laws in India. Retrieved from https://blog.ipleaders.in/labour-laws-in-india-2/
4. Shift Workspaces. (n.d.). The Benefits of Mindfulness in the Workplace. Retrieved from https://shiftworkspaces.com/the-benefits-of-mindfulness-in-the-workplace/

Chapter 19: Education and Skill Development

The dharmic economy requires a holistic approach to education and skill development that emphasizes lifelong learning, adaptability, and the integration of ethics and values. This chapter explores holistic education models, the importance of continuous learning, and strategies for incorporating ethical principles into professional training.

Holistic Education Models for the Dharmic Economy

Holistic education is an approach that focuses on developing the whole person, addressing not just academic knowledge but also emotional, social, physical, and spiritual aspects of an individual. This aligns closely with dharmic principles that emphasize the interconnectedness of all aspects of life and the importance of balance and harmony.

Key principles of holistic education include:
1. Interconnectedness: Recognizing the relationships between different subjects and between academic learning and real-world applications.
2. Wholeness: Viewing the student as a whole person with diverse needs and potentials.
3. Transformation: Focusing on personal growth and development rather than just the acquisition of information.
4. Experiential learning: Emphasizing hands-on experiences and real-world applications of knowledge.
According to New Horizon Gurukul, holistic education offers several benefits:

- Improves critical-thinking and problem-solving skills
- Promotes introspection and builds self-confidence
- Encourages creativity

- Provides opportunities to explore new things
- Fosters self-directed learning
- Develops essential skills like responsibility, empathy, and collaboration

Several educational models support holistic education:

1. Montessori: This method focuses on hands-on learning that combines playing, learning, and exploring new things independently.
2. Waldorf: Following the 3H principle (head, heart, and hands), this approach involves a holistic learning method.
3. Project-based learning: This approach enhances critical thinking and teamwork skills.
4. Integrated thematic instruction: Linking diverse subjects to provide a more comprehensive understanding.
5. Experiential learning: Providing hands-on experiences to reinforce theoretical concepts.
6. Service learning: Developing traits like empathy and responsibility through community engagement.
7. Mindfulness and wellness programs: Facilitating self-reflection and self-awareness.

Implementing holistic education in the classroom involves several strategies:
1. Creating a supportive and conducive environment for personal growth and development.
2. Providing customized teaching based on individual strengths and weaknesses to boost self-confidence.
3. Encouraging self-reflection and mindfulness practices.
4. Offering praise and recognition to reinforce positive behaviors and boost self-esteem.
5. Implementing project-based learning and integrated thematic instruction to enhance critical thinking and teamwork skills.
6. Incorporating mindfulness and wellness programs to facilitate self-awareness and emotional regulation.

By adopting these holistic education models and strategies, educational institutions can better prepare students for the complexities of the dharmic economy, fostering not just academic excellence but also personal growth, ethical decision-making, and social responsibility.

Lifelong Learning and Adaptability

In the rapidly evolving landscape of the modern economy, lifelong learning and adaptability have become essential skills. The concept of lifelong learning aligns closely with dharmic principles of continuous self-improvement and adaptation to changing circumstances.

According to a study on lifelong learning, it is defined as learning "from cradle to grave" and is a philosophy, conceptual framework, and organizing principle of all forms of education. It encompasses formal, informal, and non-formal learning experiences encountered throughout one's lifetime.

Key aspects of lifelong learning include:

1. Continuous skill development: Regularly upgrading competencies to meet changing workplace demands.
2. Adaptability: Developing the ability to learn new skills quickly and apply them in different contexts.
3. Self-directed learning: Taking initiative in identifying learning needs and pursuing relevant knowledge and skills.
4. Interdisciplinary approach: Combining knowledge from different fields to solve complex problems.
5. Embracing technology: Utilizing digital tools and platforms for learning and skill development.

The importance of lifelong learning has increased due to several factors:

1. Rapid technological advancements: The fast pace of technological change requires continuous updating of skills and

knowledge.
2. Globalization: The interconnected global economy demands adaptability and cross-cultural competencies.
3. Changing job market: Many careers now require multiple skill sets and the ability to pivot to new roles.
4. Increasing life expectancy: Longer lifespans mean individuals may have multiple careers over their lifetime.

To promote lifelong learning and adaptability, educational institutions and organizations can:
1. Offer flexible learning options: Provide a variety of learning formats, including online courses, workshops, and mentorship programs.
2. Encourage a growth mindset: Foster a culture that values continuous learning and sees challenges as opportunities for growth.
3. Develop metacognitive skills: Teach students how to learn effectively and self-assess their learning needs.
4. Emphasize transferable skills: Focus on developing skills that can be applied across different contexts and industries.
5. Integrate technology: Incorporate digital literacy and technological skills into all aspects of education and training.
6. Promote interdisciplinary learning: Encourage students to explore connections between different fields of study.
7. Partner with industry: Collaborate with businesses to ensure educational programs align with current and future workforce needs.

By embracing lifelong learning and adaptability, individuals can better navigate the complexities of the dharmic economy, continuously evolving their skills and knowledge to meet changing demands and contribute positively to society.

Integrating Ethics and Values in Professional Training

Responsible dharmic economy leaders and practitioners must be nurtured via professional training that incorporates ethics and values. As a result of this integration, people are prepared to make ethical judgments in their careers, in addition to having the technical abilities that are required.

It is impossible to overestimate the significance of ethical behavior in the intricate corporate world, according to a research on incorporating ethical practices into business education. It is the responsibility of business schools to instill in its pupils the values and concepts that will enable them to conduct themselves responsibly in the corporate world.

Key aspects of integrating ethics and values in professional training include:

1. Ethical decision-making frameworks: Teaching structured approaches to analyzing ethical dilemmas and making principled decisions.
2. Case studies and real-world examples: Using actual scenarios to illustrate ethical challenges and discuss potential solutions.
3. Stakeholder analysis: Encouraging consideration of the impact of decisions on all stakeholders, not just shareholders.
4. Corporate social responsibility: Emphasizing the role of businesses in contributing positively to society and the environment.
5. Professional codes of conduct: Familiarizing students with industry-specific ethical standards and expectations.
6. Personal values clarification: Helping individuals identify and articulate their own ethical principles and how they align with professional expectations.
7. Ethical leadership: Developing skills for promoting and maintaining ethical cultures within organizations.

Strategies for implementing ethics and values in professional training:
1. Standalone ethics courses: Offering dedicated courses on business ethics and professional responsibility.
2. Integration across curriculum: Incorporating ethical

considerations into all relevant courses and subjects.
3. Experiential learning: Providing opportunities for students to engage in ethical decision-making through simulations, internships, and service-learning projects.
4. Guest speakers and mentorship: Inviting industry professionals to share their experiences with ethical challenges and decision-making.
5. Ethics committees and honor codes: Establishing student-led initiatives to promote ethical behavior within educational institutions.
6. Reflective practices: Encouraging journaling, group discussions, and self-assessment to deepen understanding of personal and professional ethics.
7. Interdisciplinary approaches: Collaborating with philosophy, sociology, and psychology departments to provide a broader perspective on ethical issues.

Benefits of integrating ethics and values in professional training:
1. Enhanced decision-making skills: Developing the ability to navigate complex ethical dilemmas in professional settings.
2. Improved reputation management: Understanding the importance of ethical behavior in maintaining personal and organizational reputation.
3. Increased stakeholder trust: Fostering relationships built on integrity and transparency with customers, employees, and communities.
4. Risk mitigation: Identifying and addressing potential ethical risks before they escalate into crises.
5. Positive organizational culture: Contributing to workplaces that value integrity, respect, and social responsibility.
6. Long-term sustainability: Recognizing the role of ethical practices in ensuring the long-term viability of businesses and industries.

By integrating ethics and values into professional training, educational institutions can prepare students to become responsible leaders who understand the impact of their decisions on society, foster a culture of integrity, and ensure sustainable business practices that benefit both the organization and the broader community.

References:
1. https://newhorizongurukul.in/4-pillars-of-holistic-education-2/
2. https://islamicstudies.uok.edu.in/Files/36892408-1fed-4431-9848-0761b9e02587/Journal/34aee698-57dc-43a6-bc37-155cd76a27c1.pdf
3. https://flearningstudio.com/5-examples-ethics-training-programs/
4. https://soeonline.american.edu/blog/what-is-holistic-education/
5. https://hrcak.srce.hr/ojs/index.php/entrenova/article/view/33640
6. https://www.chitkara.edu.in/blogs/integrating-ethical-practices-in-business-education/
7. https://www.teacheracademy.eu/blog/holistic-education/

Chapter 20: Artificial Intelligence and the Future of Work

The rapid advancement of artificial intelligence (AI) is reshaping the landscape of work and society, bringing both immense opportunities and profound ethical challenges. This chapter explores the ethical considerations in AI development, examines approaches to balancing technological progress with human values, and discusses how dharmic principles can guide our preparation for potential job displacement.

Ethical Considerations in AI Development

As AI systems become increasingly sophisticated and ubiquitous, ensuring their ethical development and deployment has become a critical concern. Several key ethical issues have emerged as central to the responsible advancement of AI technology:

Bias and Fairness: One of the primary ethical challenges in AI development is addressing bias and ensuring fairness. AI algorithms learn from historical data, which may contain inherent biases reflecting societal prejudices. If these biases are not identified and mitigated, AI systems can perpetuate and amplify discrimination, leading to unfair outcomes across various domains, from hiring practices to criminal justice (Merit Data & Technology, n.d.).

To address this issue, ethical AI development must involve:
- Auditing training data for biases
- Monitoring model performance across different demographic groups
- Implementing fairness-aware algorithms during model training

- Regularly assessing AI systems for discriminatory outcomes

Transparency and Explainability: Many AI models, particularly deep learning systems, operate as "black boxes," making it difficult to understand their decision-making processes. This lack of transparency raises concerns about accountability and trust in AI systems. Ethical AI development requires prioritizing transparency and explainability by:
- Choosing interpretable models when possible
- Providing clear explanations for model predictions
- Documenting model behavior and limitations
- Developing techniques to make complex AI systems more understandable to users and stakeholders

Privacy Protection: AI systems often process vast amounts of personal data, raising significant privacy concerns. Ethical AI development must prioritize robust privacy protection measures, including:
- Implementing privacy-enhancing techniques such as differential privacy and federated learning
- Minimizing data collection and retention
- Ensuring informed consent for data usage
- Complying with data protection regulations and best practices

Accountability and Responsibility: As AI systems become more autonomous in their decision-making, questions of accountability and responsibility become increasingly complex. Ethical AI development requires establishing clear lines of responsibility for AI outcomes and implementing mechanisms for human oversight. This may involve:
- Designing human-in-the-loop systems for critical decisions
- Establishing clear protocols for escalating complex cases to human experts
- Developing frameworks for assigning legal and ethical responsibility for AI actions

Safety and Robustness: Ensuring the safety and reliability of AI systems is crucial, especially as they are deployed in high-stakes domains such as healthcare and transportation. Ethical AI development must prioritize:
- Rigorous testing and validation of AI systems
- Implementing fail-safe mechanisms and fallback procedures
- Continuously monitoring and updating systems to address vulnerabilities and errors

Long-term Societal Impact: The widespread adoption of AI has the potential to transform society in profound ways. Ethical AI development requires considering the long-term societal impacts of these technologies, including:
- Potential job displacement and economic disruption
- Changes in social interactions and relationships
- Impacts on human autonomy and decision-making
- Environmental consequences of AI deployment

Addressing these ethical considerations requires a multifaceted approach involving various stakeholders, including AI developers, policymakers, ethicists, and representatives from affected communities. As noted by a Merit expert, "To operationalise ethical considerations, it's essential to define specific guidelines and principles for each project, aligning them with broader ethical principles such as fairness, transparency, and privacy" (Merit Data & Technology, n.d.).

Balancing Technological Progress with Human Values

As AI technology continues to advance at a rapid pace, finding a balance between technological progress and human values has become increasingly crucial. This balance is essential not only for ethical reasons but also for ensuring the long-term sustainability and acceptance of AI systems in society.

Integrating Human Values into AI Development:

One approach to balancing technological progress with human values is to explicitly incorporate ethical considerations and human-centered principles into the AI development process. This can involve:

1. Value Alignment: Designing AI systems that are aligned with human values and ethical principles. This requires ongoing dialogue between AI developers, ethicists, and diverse stakeholder groups to identify and prioritize relevant values.
2. Ethical Impact Assessments: Conducting thorough assessments of the potential ethical impacts of AI systems before deployment, considering effects on various stakeholders and societal groups.
3. Interdisciplinary Collaboration: Fostering collaboration between AI researchers, social scientists, ethicists, and policymakers to ensure a holistic approach to AI development that considers technical, social, and ethical dimensions.
4. Human-Centered Design: Prioritizing user needs, preferences, and well-being in the design of AI systems, ensuring that technology serves human interests rather than the other way around.

Regulatory Frameworks and Governance: Developing appropriate regulatory frameworks and governance structures is crucial for balancing technological progress with human values. This may involve:
1. Ethical Guidelines: Establishing clear ethical guidelines and standards for AI development and deployment, such as the European Union's Ethics Guidelines for Trustworthy AI.
2. Regulatory Oversight: Creating regulatory bodies to monitor AI development and ensure compliance with ethical standards and legal requirements.
3. International Cooperation: Fostering global collaboration to develop harmonized approaches to AI governance, addressing cross-border challenges and ensuring consistent ethical standards.
4. Adaptive Regulation: Implementing flexible regulatory

frameworks that can evolve alongside rapid technological advancements while maintaining core ethical principles.

Public Engagement and Education: Engaging the public in discussions about AI ethics and fostering AI literacy is essential for balancing technological progress with societal values. This can include:

1. Public Dialogue: Organizing forums and platforms for public discussion on the ethical implications of AI technologies.
2. AI Education: Developing educational programs to improve public understanding of AI technologies, their potential impacts, and ethical considerations.
3. Participatory Design: Involving diverse stakeholders, including potential end-users, in the design and development process of AI systems.
4. Transparency Initiatives: Promoting transparency in AI development and deployment, enabling public scrutiny and fostering trust.

Ethical Business Practices: Companies developing and deploying AI technologies have a crucial role in balancing progress with human values. This involves:

1. Corporate Social Responsibility: Integrating ethical considerations into corporate decision-making processes and business strategies.
2. Ethical AI Teams: Establishing dedicated teams or committees within organizations to address ethical issues in AI development and deployment.
3. Responsible Innovation: Adopting principles of responsible innovation that consider the broader societal impacts of AI technologies.
4. Stakeholder Engagement: Actively engaging with diverse stakeholders to understand and address concerns related to AI deployment.

By implementing these strategies, we can work towards a future where AI technology advances in harmony with human values, contributing to societal well-being while mitigating potential risks and ethical concerns.

Preparing for Job Displacement through Dharmic Principles

The potential for widespread job displacement due to AI and automation is a significant concern as we look to the future of work. Dharmic principles offer valuable insights for addressing this challenge in an ethical and sustainable manner.

Dharma and Adaptability: The concept of dharma emphasizes fulfilling one's duties and responsibilities in alignment with cosmic order. In the context of job displacement, this principle encourages individuals to adapt to changing circumstances and find new ways to contribute to society. Key aspects include:
1. Lifelong Learning: Embracing continuous education and skill development to remain relevant in a rapidly changing job market.
2. Flexibility: Being open to new career paths and opportunities that may arise from technological advancements.
3. Service Orientation: Focusing on how one's skills and talents can be applied to serve others and contribute to the greater good, even as traditional job roles evolve.

Karma and Personal Responsibility: The principle of karma emphasizes the importance of taking responsibility for one's actions and their consequences. In preparing for potential job displacement, this can translate to:
1. Proactive Skill Development: Taking initiative to acquire new skills and knowledge in anticipation of future job market needs.
2. Ethical Decision-Making: Making career choices that align with one's values and contribute positively to society, even in the face of technological disruption.
3. Resilience: Developing mental and emotional resilience to navigate career transitions and setbacks.

Ahimsa and Compassionate Transition: The principle of ahimsa (non-violence) can guide approaches to managing job

displacement in a way that minimizes harm and promotes social harmony:
1. Gradual Transition: Implementing AI and automation technologies in a phased manner to allow for smoother workforce transitions.
2. Retraining Programs: Developing comprehensive retraining and reskilling programs to help displaced workers find new employment opportunities.
3. Social Safety Nets: Advocating for and supporting social safety net programs to assist those affected by job displacement.

Aparigraha and Sustainable Economics: The principle of aparigraha (non-possessiveness) encourages a more sustainable and equitable approach to economic development:
1. Shared Prosperity: Exploring models of shared ownership and profit-sharing to ensure the benefits of AI-driven productivity gains are distributed more widely.
2. Alternative Economic Models: Considering alternative economic frameworks, such as universal basic income or universal basic services, to address potential long-term unemployment challenges.
3. Focus on Well-being: Shifting economic priorities from pure profit maximization to holistic measures of societal well-being and sustainable development.

As we navigate the complex ethical landscape of AI development and its impact on the future of work, integrating dharmic principles with modern ethical frameworks offers a promising approach. By prioritizing transparency, fairness, and human values in AI development, we can harness the potential of these technologies while mitigating their risks. Simultaneously, applying dharmic concepts to workforce preparation and economic restructuring can help create a more resilient, adaptable, and ethically grounded approach to managing the transitions ahead.

The challenges posed by AI and automation are significant, but they also present an opportunity to reimagine our economic systems and societal structures in ways that promote greater equity, sustainability, and human flourishing. By balancing technological progress with enduring human values and ethical principles, we can work towards a future where AI serves as a tool for empowerment and positive social transformation.

References:
1. https://www.meritdata-tech.com/resources/blog/code-ai/ai-ethics-privacy-accountability/
2. https://www.coe.int/en/web/bioethics/common-ethical-challenges-in-ai
3. https://drpress.org/ojs/index.php/ijeh/article/view/22205
4. https://www.ramana-maharshi.org/dharma-in-the-workplace-hinduism-and-business-ethics/
5. https://positivepsychology.com/mindfulness-at-work/
6. https://swarajyamag.com/economy/anna-yojana-is-modis-pragmatic-alternative-to-universal-basic-income

Chapter 21: Dharmic Governance Models

The concept of dharmic governance offers valuable insights for addressing the challenges of modern political systems. By applying ancient principles of righteous rulership, participatory democracy, and accountability to contemporary contexts, we can envision more ethical and effective models of governance. This chapter explores how raja dharma can inform modern governance practices, examines approaches to participatory democracy and decentralization, and discusses strategies for enhancing transparency and accountability in public institutions.

Applying Raja Dharma (Righteous Rulership) to Modern Governance

The ancient Indian concept of raja dharma, or the duty of righteous rulership, provides a comprehensive ethical framework that can inform modern governance practices. Raja dharma emphasizes that rulers have a moral obligation to prioritize the welfare of their subjects and uphold principles of justice, fairness, and integrity.

Key principles of raja dharma that can be applied to modern governance include:

1. Prioritizing public welfare: Raja dharma emphasizes that the primary duty of a ruler is to ensure the well-being and prosperity of the people. This aligns closely with modern concepts of good governance focused on public service and social welfare.

2. Ethical leadership: Rulers are expected to lead by example, embodying virtues such as honesty, compassion, and self-discipline. This principle underscores the importance of ethical

conduct among political leaders and public officials.

3. Impartial justice: Raja dharma stresses the need for rulers to administer justice fairly and impartially, regardless of an individual's social status. This principle resonates with modern ideals of equality before the law and due process.

4. Protection of the vulnerable: Ancient texts emphasize the ruler's duty to protect the weak and vulnerable members of society. This aligns with modern social welfare policies and human rights protections.

5. Balancing authority with responsibility: While raja dharma recognizes the authority of rulers, it also emphasizes their accountability to dharma (ethical principles) and the welfare of the people. This balance between power and responsibility is crucial in modern democratic systems.

Implementing raja dharma principles in modern governance could involve:

1. Ethical training for public officials: Incorporating ethics education and training programs for politicians and civil servants based on raja dharma principles.

2. Performance metrics based on public welfare: Developing governance evaluation systems that prioritize measures of social well-being and equitable development.

3. Strengthening anti-corruption measures: Implementing robust systems to prevent and punish corruption in public office, aligning with the raja dharma emphasis on ethical conduct.

4. Inclusive policy-making: Ensuring that governance processes consider the needs of all segments of society, particularly the most vulnerable.

5. Long-term planning: Encouraging political leaders to focus on long-term societal benefits rather than short-term political

gains.

The application of raja dharma to modern governance is not without challenges. Critics may argue that ancient concepts are not directly applicable to complex modern societies. However, the core ethical principles of raja dharma – prioritizing public welfare, ethical leadership, and accountability – remain highly relevant to addressing contemporary governance challenges.

Participatory Democracy and Decentralization

Participatory democracy and decentralization are key components of dharmic governance models, aligning with the principle of involving citizens in decision-making processes that affect their lives. These approaches can enhance the responsiveness and accountability of governance systems.

Participatory democracy involves creating mechanisms for direct citizen involvement in policy-making and governance beyond periodic elections. Key aspects include:

1. Citizen consultations: Regular forums for citizens to provide input on policy decisions and local governance issues.

2. Participatory budgeting: Allowing citizens to have a direct say in allocating a portion of public budgets to local priorities.

3. Citizen assemblies: Randomly selected groups of citizens deliberating on specific policy issues and making recommendations.

4. Digital participation platforms: Leveraging technology to enable broader citizen engagement in governance processes.

Decentralization involves devolving decision-making power from central authorities to local levels. This aligns with dharmic principles of subsidiarity – addressing issues at the most immediate level consistent with their resolution. Key aspects of decentralization include:

1. Administrative decentralization: Transferring responsibility for planning, financing, and managing certain public functions to local authorities.

2. Fiscal decentralization: Providing local governments with the authority to raise and retain financial resources.

3. Political decentralization: Giving citizens and their elected representatives more power in public decision-making.

The benefits of participatory democracy and decentralization include:

1. Increased responsiveness to local needs: Local decision-making can better address community-specific issues.

2. Enhanced accountability: Closer proximity between citizens and decision-makers can improve oversight and reduce corruption.

3. Improved policy outcomes: Incorporating diverse local knowledge and perspectives can lead to more effective and tailored solutions.

4. Increased civic engagement: Direct participation can foster a more active and informed citizenry.

5. Conflict resolution: Local-level decision-making can help manage conflicts and build consensus within communities.

Implementing participatory democracy and decentralization requires careful consideration of institutional design and capacity building. Key challenges include:

1. Ensuring equitable participation: Preventing the domination of participatory processes by elite or more vocal groups.

2. Balancing local and national interests: Maintaining coherent national policies while empowering local decision-making.

3. Building local capacity: Ensuring local governments have

the skills and resources to effectively manage devolved responsibilities.

4. Overcoming resistance: Addressing potential resistance from central authorities reluctant to cede power.

Successful examples of participatory democracy and decentralization can be found in various contexts. For instance, the participatory budgeting process pioneered in Porto Alegre, Brazil, has been adopted in numerous cities worldwide, demonstrating the potential for scaling up participatory approaches.

Transparency and Accountability in Public Institutions

Transparency and accountability are fundamental principles of dharmic governance, aligning with the emphasis on ethical conduct and public trust in leadership. In modern contexts, these principles are crucial for ensuring effective and responsible governance.

Key aspects of transparency in public institutions include:

1. Access to information: Ensuring citizens have easy access to government data, policies, and decision-making processes.

2. Open government initiatives: Proactively sharing government information and data in user-friendly formats.

3. Transparent budgeting: Providing clear, understandable information about government revenues, expenditures, and financial management.

4. Public procurement transparency: Ensuring open and fair processes for government contracts and purchases.

Accountability measures in public institutions may include:

1. Performance audits: Regular evaluations of government programs and agencies to assess effectiveness and efficiency.

2. Whistleblower protections: Safeguarding individuals who report misconduct or corruption in public institutions.

3. Independent oversight bodies: Establishing agencies like ombudsmen or anti-corruption commissions to investigate complaints and monitor government activities.

4. Citizen feedback mechanisms: Creating channels for citizens to report issues and provide input on public services.

Implementing transparency and accountability measures can lead to several benefits:

1. Increased public trust: Open and accountable governance can enhance citizens' confidence in public institutions.

2. Improved efficiency: Transparency can help identify and address inefficiencies in government operations.

3. Reduced corruption: Open processes and strong accountability measures can deter and detect corrupt practices.

4. Better policy outcomes: Informed public scrutiny can lead to more effective and responsive policies.

5. Enhanced democratic participation: Access to information empowers citizens to engage more meaningfully in governance processes.

Challenges in implementing transparency and accountability measures include:

1. Balancing transparency with privacy and security concerns: Ensuring open government does not compromise sensitive personal or national security information.

2. Overcoming bureaucratic resistance: Addressing potential reluctance within government agencies to increase transparency.

3. Ensuring accessibility: Making information available in

formats and languages that are accessible to all citizens.

4. Managing information overload: Providing clear, relevant information without overwhelming citizens with excessive data.

Successful examples of transparency and accountability initiatives can be found in various countries. For instance, Estonia's e-governance system provides citizens with comprehensive online access to government services and information, demonstrating the potential of digital technologies in enhancing transparency.

Dharmic governance models offer valuable insights for addressing the challenges of modern political systems. By applying principles of raja dharma to contemporary contexts, we can envision governance approaches that prioritize ethical leadership, public welfare, and long-term societal benefits. Participatory democracy and decentralization align with dharmic emphasis on inclusive decision-making and community empowerment, offering pathways to more responsive and accountable governance. Finally, transparency and accountability measures are crucial for ensuring that public institutions operate ethically and effectively in service of the common good.

As we navigate the complex governance challenges of the 21st century, integrating these dharmic principles with modern democratic practices offers a promising approach to creating more ethical, responsive, and effective systems of governance. While implementation may face challenges, the potential benefits in terms of enhanced public trust, improved policy outcomes, and more engaged citizenry make this an endeavor worth pursuing.

References

Adikka Channels. (n.d.). Rajadharma And Rakshadharma:

Key Aspects Of Governance And Protection In Sanatana Dharma. https://adikkachannels.com/rajadharma-and-rakshadharma-key-aspects-of-governance-and-protection-in-sanatana-dharma/

Council of Europe. (n.d.). About participatory democracy. https://www.coe.int/en/web/participatory-democracy/about-participatory-democracy

Development Monitoring and Evaluation Office. (n.d.). Accountability and Transparency in Governance. https://dmeo.gov.in/sites/default/files/2022-04/Thematic_Report_Accountability_and_Transparency_22042022.pdf

India Foundation. (n.d.). Rājadharma: The Bhāratīya Notion of Welfare State. https://indiafoundation.in/articles-and-commentaries/rajadharma-the-bharatiya-notion-of-welfare-state/

iPleaders. (n.d.). Labour laws in India. https://blog.ipleaders.in/labour-laws-in-india-2/

Patsias, C., & Patsias, S. (n.d.). Participatory Democracy, Decentralization and Local Governance. https://www.oidp.net/docs/repo/doc932.pdf

Sharma, M. (n.d.). Learning Lessons from Raj Dharma: The Concept of Good Governance. Indian Journal of Law, Polity and Administration. https://www.ijlpa.com/_files/ugd/006c7e_271ad69e99774f54bde013642584a88a.pdf

Chapter 22: Economic Policy Through a Dharmic Lens

Economic policy plays a crucial role in shaping the well-being of societies and individuals. When viewed through a dharmic lens, economic policy takes on additional ethical dimensions that emphasize balance, sustainability, and holistic measures of progress. This chapter explores how dharmic principles can inform approaches to balancing free market principles with social welfare, aligning environmental regulations with dharmic values, and measuring national progress beyond traditional GDP metrics.

Balancing Free Market Principles with Social Welfare

The tension between free market principles and social welfare considerations is a central challenge in economic policy. A dharmic perspective offers valuable insights for finding a middle path that harnesses the efficiency of markets while ensuring social equity and well-being.

Buddhist economics, as outlined by scholars, provides a framework for understanding this balance. The purpose of economic activity in Buddhism is to provide the necessary material basis for individuals to enjoy life, freeing them to pursue higher forms of well-being. Production, consumption, and distribution of material goods should reduce suffering and provide sustainable welfare and dignified work for all members of society[1].

This view contrasts with classical Western economics, which often focuses on maximizing individual utility or welfare through ever-increasing material production. Buddhist economics treats economic life as part of living in accordance with dharma, viewing it as part of a larger whole that must be kept in harmony with familial, social, environmental, and spiritual aspects of life[1].

Key principles for balancing free market dynamics with social welfare include:

1. Recognizing the interconnectedness of economic activities: Buddhist economics acknowledges that there are no true "externalities" - all economic actions have broader societal impacts that must be considered[1].

2. Prioritizing basic needs: The state should guarantee the "four essentials" of food, clothing, shelter, and medicine as a foundation for other pursuits[1].

3. Ethical wealth creation: While not anti-wealth, Buddhist economics emphasizes creating prosperity through ethical means that benefit society[1].

4. Role of government: A somewhat greater role for the state in economic affairs is envisioned, similar to welfare liberalism in advanced market economies[1].

5. Mixed market approach: Markets are seen as effective for many purposes, but not the answer to all economic problems. Government has a responsibility to uphold societal values beyond just liberty and efficiency[1].

Implementing these principles in modern economic policy could involve:

1. Progressive taxation and robust social safety nets to ensure basic needs are met for all citizens.

2. Regulations to internalize externalities, ensuring businesses account for their full societal and environmental impacts.

3. Incentives for ethical business practices and corporate social responsibility initiatives.

4. Public investment in essential infrastructure, education, and

healthcare to provide a foundation for individual and societal flourishing.

5. Policies to promote fair labor practices and dignified work opportunities.

The dharmic approach to balancing markets and social welfare aligns with emerging concepts of "conscious capitalism" and stakeholder-oriented business models. By recognizing the interconnectedness of economic activities and their broader impacts, this perspective encourages a more holistic and sustainable approach to economic policy.

Environmental Regulations Aligned with Dharmic Values

Environmental protection is a critical concern in modern economic policy, and dharmic principles offer valuable guidance for developing regulations that promote ecological balance and sustainability. The dharmic worldview emphasizes the interconnectedness of all beings and the importance of living in harmony with nature.

Key dharmic values relevant to environmental regulations include:

1. Ahimsa (non-violence): Extending the principle of non-harm to encompass the natural world and ecosystems.

2. Aparigraha (non-possessiveness): Encouraging sustainable resource use and discouraging overconsumption.

3. Karma: Recognizing the long-term consequences of environmental actions and policies.

4. Interconnectedness: Acknowledging the complex relationships between human activities and natural systems.

Applying these principles to environmental regulations could involve:

1. Comprehensive environmental impact assessments:

Requiring thorough evaluations of the ecological consequences of economic activities and development projects.

2. Circular economy initiatives: Promoting closed-loop production systems that minimize waste and maximize resource efficiency.

3. Biodiversity protection: Implementing strong measures to preserve ecosystems and protect endangered species.

4. Renewable energy transition: Accelerating the shift to clean energy sources to mitigate climate change impacts.

5. Sustainable agriculture practices: Encouraging farming methods that preserve soil health, protect water resources, and promote biodiversity.

6. Extended producer responsibility: Holding manufacturers accountable for the entire lifecycle of their products, including disposal and recycling.

The dharmic emphasis on interconnectedness aligns with modern ecological understanding and supports a systems-thinking approach to environmental policy. This perspective encourages policymakers to consider the complex interactions between economic activities and natural systems, leading to more comprehensive and effective environmental regulations.

Measuring National Progress Beyond GDP

Traditional measures of economic progress, particularly Gross Domestic Product (GDP), have long been criticized for their limitations in capturing true societal well-being and sustainability. A dharmic approach to measuring national progress emphasizes a more holistic view that considers social, environmental, and spiritual dimensions alongside economic factors.

The limitations of GDP as a measure of progress include:

1. Failure to account for environmental degradation and resource depletion[4].
2. Inability to capture the value of unpaid work, such as household labor[4].
3. Lack of consideration for income inequality and distribution[4].
4. Exclusion of non-market activities that contribute to well-being[4].

Several alternative measures have been developed to address these shortcomings:

1. Human Development Index (HDI): Created by the United Nations, the HDI focuses on people and their capabilities rather than economic growth alone. It considers health, education, and standard of living[5].

2. Better Life Index: Developed by the OECD, this index allows users to compare well-being across countries based on 11 topics identified as essential[5].

3. Genuine Progress Indicator (GPI): This measure accounts for economic, environmental, and social factors, including variables such as income inequality, environmental degradation, and volunteer work[5].

4. Gross National Happiness (GNH): Pioneered by Bhutan, GNH measures progress in terms of sustainable development, cultural values, natural environment, and good governance[2].

Implementing a more holistic measure of national progress aligned with dharmic principles could involve:

1. Developing a comprehensive framework that integrates economic, social, environmental, and spiritual indicators.

2. Incorporating measures of community capital - natural, social, human, and built - to assess sustainable development[4].

3. Including indicators of ethical conduct and spiritual well-being in national assessments.

4. Emphasizing long-term sustainability and intergenerational equity in progress metrics.

5. Measuring the degree to which society's goals (e.g., providing basic human needs, fostering participation) are met, rather than just the volume of economic activity[4].

The United Nations has recognized the need for more comprehensive measures of progress. UN Secretary-General António Guterres has proposed developing complementary metrics to GDP that more fully recognize what matters to people, the planet, and our future[6]. His proposals include:

1. Creating a conceptual framework to "value what counts" for people, the planet, and the future, anchored in the 2030 Agenda.
2. Elaborating a UN value dashboard featuring key indicators that go beyond GDP.
3. Launching a capacity-building initiative to enable countries to use the new framework effectively[6].

By adopting more holistic measures of progress aligned with dharmic principles, policymakers can gain a more accurate understanding of societal well-being and make more informed decisions that promote true sustainable development.

Viewing economic policy through a dharmic lens offers valuable insights for addressing the complex challenges of the 21st century. By balancing free market principles with social welfare considerations, aligning environmental regulations with dharmic values, and adopting more comprehensive measures of national progress, policymakers can work towards creating economic systems that promote both material prosperity and holistic well-being.

The dharmic emphasis on interconnectedness, ethical conduct, and long-term sustainability provides a framework for developing policies that address the root causes of economic, social, and environmental challenges. As we face growing global issues such as inequality, climate change, and social fragmentation, integrating dharmic wisdom with modern economic practices offers a promising path towards more equitable, sustainable, and fulfilling economic systems.

Moving forward, further research and practical experimentation will be crucial to refine and implement these concepts in diverse cultural and economic contexts. By continuing to explore the intersection of ancient wisdom and contemporary economic challenges, we can work towards creating economies that not only generate wealth but also foster human flourishing and ecological balance.

References

1. Costanza, R., Hart, M., Posner, S., & Talberth, J. (n.d.). Beyond GDP: The Need for New Measures of Progress. Boston University. https://www.bu.edu/pardee/files/documents/PP-004-GDP.pdf
2. Guterres, A. (n.d.). Valuing What Counts: Framework to Progress Beyond Gross Domestic Product. LinkedIn. https://www.linkedin.com/pulse/valuing-what-counts-framework-to-progress-beyond-gross-domestic-product-guterres
3. Sharma, S. (n.d.). Free Market Dharma. The Caravan. https://caravanmagazine.in/reviews-essays/free-market-dharma
4. St. Louis Fed. (2023, April). Beyond GDP: Three Other Ways to Measure Economic Health. https://www.stlouisfed.org/open-vault/2023/apr/three-other-ways-to-measure-economic-health-beyond-gdp
5. World Economic Forum. (2024, September 24). The shift to new and nature-positive measures of progress. https://

www.weforum.org/stories/2024/09/beyond-gdp-nature-positive-measures-progress-gaining-momentum/

6. Zadek, S. (n.d.). Buddha on Politics, Economics, and Statecraft. SpringerLink. https://link.springer.com/chapter/10.1007/978-3-030-68042-8_3

Chapter 23: Global Cooperation and Trade

In an increasingly interconnected world, the principles of dharma offer valuable insights for fostering global cooperation, promoting fair trade, and addressing shared challenges. This chapter explores how dharmic concepts can inform international relations, guide the development of equitable trade agreements, and inspire collective action on global issues.

Dharmic Principles in International Relations

The application of dharmic principles to international relations provides a framework for promoting peace, mutual understanding, and ethical conduct between nations. Several key dharmic concepts are particularly relevant to the realm of global diplomacy and cooperation:

1. Ahimsa (non-violence): In international relations, ahimsa encourages peaceful conflict resolution and diplomacy over aggression or military action. This principle aligns with the United Nations' emphasis on peaceful settlement of disputes and the prohibition of the use of force in international relations.
2. Satya (truthfulness): Applied to diplomacy, satya promotes transparency, honesty, and trust-building between nations. This can foster more open and productive international dialogues and negotiations.
3. Vasudhaiva Kutumbakam (the world is one family): This concept encourages a global perspective that recognizes the interconnectedness of all nations and peoples. It promotes international cooperation and solidarity in addressing shared challenges.
4. Karma (action and its consequences): In the context of international relations, karma emphasizes the long-term

consequences of a nation's actions on the global stage. This principle encourages responsible and ethical foreign policy decisions.

5. Dharma (duty/righteousness): Applied to international conduct, dharma suggests that nations have ethical obligations and responsibilities within the global community.

The relevance of these principles to modern international relations is evident in various diplomatic initiatives and frameworks. For example, the five principles of peaceful coexistence, also known as Panchsheel, which have been influential in Asian diplomacy, share similarities with dharmic concepts:

1. Mutual respect for territorial integrity and sovereignty
2. Mutual non-aggression
3. Mutual non-interference in internal affairs
4. Equality and mutual benefit
5. Peaceful coexistence

These principles align closely with dharmic values of non-violence, respect, and mutual cooperation[1].

Implementing dharmic principles in international relations could involve:

1. Prioritizing diplomatic solutions and multilateral cooperation in addressing global challenges.
2. Developing more inclusive and equitable global governance structures that reflect the principle of vasudhaiva kutumbakam.
3. Promoting transparency and ethical conduct in international negotiations and agreements.
4. Emphasizing long-term, sustainable approaches to global development and environmental protection.
5. Fostering cultural exchange and dialogue to promote mutual understanding between nations.

By incorporating these dharmic principles into international relations, nations can work towards a more peaceful, cooperative, and ethically-grounded global order.

Fair Trade Agreements and Global Economic Justice

The concept of fair trade aligns closely with dharmic principles of justice, equity, and mutual benefit. Dharmic approaches to international trade emphasize the importance of creating economic relationships that are not merely transactional but contribute to the well-being of all parties involved.

Key dharmic principles relevant to fair trade include:
1. Samana (equality): Promoting equal opportunities and fair treatment for all participants in the global economy.
2. Karuna (compassion): Considering the welfare of vulnerable populations and developing nations in trade negotiations.
3. Aparigraha (non-possessiveness): Encouraging sustainable resource use and discouraging exploitative economic practices.

Implementing these principles in international trade agreements could involve:

1. Ensuring fair labor standards and workers' rights protections across global supply chains.
2. Incorporating environmental sustainability requirements into trade agreements.
3. Providing special provisions and support for developing nations to participate equitably in global trade.
4. Promoting technology transfer and capacity building to reduce economic disparities between nations.
5. Establishing transparent dispute resolution mechanisms that consider the interests of all stakeholders.

The United Nations Conference on Trade and Development (UNCTAD) has emphasized the need for more inclusive and sustainable trade policies. Their approach aligns with dharmic principles by advocating for trade agreements that:

1. Support economic diversification in developing countries
2. Promote sustainable and inclusive development

3. Enhance the participation of small and medium-sized enterprises in global trade
4. Address inequalities and promote inclusive growth

By incorporating these dharmic-inspired principles into trade agreements, nations can work towards a more equitable and sustainable global economic system that benefits all participants.

Addressing Global Challenges Through Collective Action

The dharmic emphasis on interconnectedness and shared responsibility provides a strong foundation for addressing global challenges through collective action. This approach recognizes that issues such as climate change, poverty, and public health crises require coordinated efforts from multiple stakeholders across national boundaries.

The concept of collective action in addressing global challenges aligns closely with the dharmic principle of sangha (community). In the context of international cooperation, this principle encourages nations to work together as a global community to tackle shared problems.

Successful collective action initiatives require several key elements:

1. Shared vision and goals: Establishing clear, common objectives that align with the interests of all participants.
2. Inclusive participation: Ensuring that all relevant stakeholders, including marginalized groups, have a voice in decision-making processes.
3. Trust-building: Fostering open communication and transparency to build trust between participants.
4. Equitable burden-sharing: Distributing responsibilities and costs fairly based on capabilities and resources.
5. Adaptive management: Implementing flexible approaches that can evolve in response to changing circumstances and new

information.

Case studies of successful collective action initiatives demonstrate the potential of this approach:

1. The Montreal Protocol on Substances that Deplete the Ozone Layer: This international treaty successfully phased out the production of ozone-depleting substances through coordinated global action.
2. The Global Polio Eradication Initiative: A public-private partnership that has reduced polio cases by 99% worldwide through collaborative efforts.
3. The Paris Agreement on Climate Change: While still ongoing, this agreement represents a significant step towards global collective action on climate change mitigation and adaptation.

These examples illustrate how collective action can effectively address complex global challenges when guided by shared goals and mutual cooperation.

To enhance the effectiveness of collective action initiatives, change-makers can:
1. Design initiatives that balance collective vision with individual innovation, allowing for diverse solutions to emerge.
2. Make agency and decentralized action guiding principles of design, striking a balance between shared goals and local implementation.
3. Foster communities of practice to facilitate cross-learning and knowledge sharing between participants.
4. Embrace principles of empowerment, inclusion, accountability, and innovation in orchestrating collective action.

By applying these dharmic-inspired approaches to collective action, the global community can more effectively address the complex, interconnected challenges of the 21st century.

The application of dharmic principles to global cooperation

and trade offers a pathway towards more ethical, equitable, and effective international relations. By emphasizing interconnectedness, mutual respect, and shared responsibility, dharmic approaches can help foster a global order that promotes peace, justice, and sustainable development.

As we face increasingly complex global challenges, from climate change to economic inequality, the wisdom embodied in dharmic traditions provides valuable guidance for creating more inclusive and effective forms of international cooperation. By integrating these principles into diplomatic practices, trade agreements, and collective action initiatives, we can work towards a more harmonious and sustainable global community.

References

1. Chavez-Segura, A. (2011). Buddhism and non-violent world: Examining a Buddhist contribution to promoting the principle of non-violence and a culture of peace. Nepal Journal of Development Studies, 5(1), 54.
2. Khushboo Awasthi Kumari, Tasso Azevedo, & Danya Pastuszek. (2024). How to orchestrate successful collective action for all. World Economic Forum. https://www.weforum.org/stories/2024/05/successfully-orchestrate-collective-action/
3. Mazzucato, M. (2023). A collective response to our global challenges: a common good and 'market-shaping' approach. UCL Institute for Innovation and Public Purpose Working Paper Series (IIPP WP 2023-2). https://www.ucl.ac.uk/bartlett/public-purpose/sites/bartlett_public_purpose/files/a_collective_response_to_our_global_challenges-_a_common_good_and_market-shaping_approach_.pdf

Chapter 24: Taxation and Public Finance

Taxation and public finance are critical components of governance that have significant implications for social equity, economic development, and the overall well-being of society. When viewed through a dharmic lens, these areas take on additional ethical dimensions that emphasize fairness, responsibility, and the promotion of collective welfare. This chapter explores ethical approaches to taxation, the allocation of public resources based on dharmic priorities, and strategies for combating corruption and promoting fiscal responsibility.

Ethical Approaches to Taxation

An ethical approach to taxation, informed by dharmic principles, emphasizes fairness, transparency, and the promotion of social good. Several key principles guide the development of an ethical tax system:

1. Equity and Fairness: The principle of equity is fundamental to an ethical tax system. As noted by Affluent CPA, "The government should exercise Equity while designing a sound tax system. Individuals should be taxed based on the amount of income they earn" (Affluent CPA, n.d.). This aligns with the dharmic concept of fairness and proportional responsibility.

2. Certainty and Simplicity: Tax laws should be clear and easily understandable to taxpayers. This principle promotes transparency and reduces the potential for confusion or unintentional non-compliance (Affluent CPA, n.d.).

3. Efficiency: An ethical tax system should minimize compliance costs for taxpayers and administrative costs for tax authorities (Affluent CPA, n.d.). This aligns with the dharmic principle of

responsible resource use.

4. Transparency: The principle of utmost good faith emphasizes transparency in tax collection and administration. As Affluent CPA states, "The government's collection of tasks should be transparent. The government should also conduct an excellent tax audit and make it available to the public" (Affluent CPA, n.d.).

5. Revenue Sufficiency: An ethical tax system should generate adequate revenue to fund necessary public services and investments (Affluent CPA, n.d.). This aligns with the dharmic concept of collective responsibility for societal well-being.

Implementing these principles in practice requires careful consideration of various tax policy elements:

1. Progressive Taxation: A progressive tax system, where tax rates increase with income, aligns with the dharmic principle of proportional responsibility. As noted in the IMF eLibrary, "The impact of a tax system on the distribution of after-tax incomes then depends on the progressivity of the tax-benefit system— that is, how rapidly the share of income taken by tax increases with the level of income" (IMF eLibrary, n.d.).

2. Broad Tax Base: Expanding the tax base while minimizing exemptions and loopholes can enhance fairness and efficiency. This approach aligns with the dharmic principle of shared responsibility for societal welfare.

3. Environmental Taxes: Incorporating environmental considerations into the tax system, such as carbon taxes or pollution charges, aligns with the dharmic principle of stewardship for the natural world.

4. Wealth Taxes: Considering taxes on wealth, in addition to income, can address issues of inequality and align with dharmic principles of non-attachment to material possessions.

5. Transparency Measures: Implementing robust reporting and

disclosure requirements for both taxpayers and tax authorities promotes accountability and trust in the tax system.

It's important to note that designing an ethical tax system involves balancing competing priorities. As the IMF eLibrary points out, "Optimal tax theory emphasizes the trade-off between equity and efficiency" (IMF eLibrary, n.d.). Finding the right balance requires careful analysis and consideration of societal values and economic realities.

Allocating Public Resources Based on Dharmic Priorities

The allocation of public resources is a critical aspect of governance that reflects a society's values and priorities. When viewed through a dharmic lens, resource allocation should prioritize collective well-being, social equity, and sustainable development.

Key dharmic principles that can guide public resource allocation include:

1. Sarvodaya (welfare of all): Prioritizing investments that benefit the broadest segments of society, particularly the most vulnerable.

2. Aparigraha (non-possessiveness): Encouraging efficient use of resources and discouraging wasteful expenditures.

3. Ahimsa (non-violence): Allocating resources to promote peace, social harmony, and environmental protection.

4. Satya (truthfulness): Ensuring transparency and accountability in the budgeting and expenditure processes.

Implementing these principles in public finance could involve:

1. Prioritizing Basic Needs: Ensuring adequate funding for essential services such as healthcare, education, and social protection. This aligns with the dharmic emphasis on collective well-being and social responsibility.

2. Sustainable Infrastructure: Investing in sustainable infrastructure projects that promote long-term economic development while minimizing environmental impact.
3. Social Equity Programs: Allocating resources to programs that address social inequalities and promote inclusive growth. This could include targeted investments in disadvantaged communities or support for marginalized groups.
4. Environmental Protection: Dedicating resources to environmental conservation, renewable energy development, and climate change mitigation efforts.
5. Participatory Budgeting: Implementing mechanisms for citizen participation in budget allocation decisions, reflecting the dharmic principle of collective responsibility.

The Development Monitoring and Evaluation Office (DMEO) of NITI Aayog emphasizes the importance of transparency and accountability in public resource allocation. They note the significance of "utilizing mechanisms like Direct Benefit Transfer, Public Financial Management Systems, Geographical Information System, social audits etc." in enhancing the effectiveness and fairness of public expenditure (DMEO, 2022).

Combating Corruption and Promoting Fiscal Responsibility

Corruption in public finance undermines the ethical foundations of governance and hinders equitable development. Promoting fiscal responsibility and combating corruption are essential for ensuring that public resources are used effectively for the benefit of society.

The International Monetary Fund (IMF) identifies several key strategies for tackling corruption in government:

1. Transparency: "Invest in high levels of transparency and independent external scrutiny. This allows audit agencies and the public at large to provide effective oversight" (IMF, 2019).

2. Institutional Reform: "Reform institutions. The chances for

success are greater when countries design reforms to tackle corruption from all angles" (IMF, 2019).

3. Professional Civil Service: "Build a professional civil service. Transparent, merit-based hiring and pay reduce the opportunities for corruption" (IMF, 2019).

4. Technology Adoption: "Keep pace with new challenges as technology and opportunities for wrongdoing evolve. Focus on areas of higher risk—such as procurement, revenue administration, and management of natural resources" (IMF, 2019).

5. International Cooperation: "Countries can also join efforts to make it harder for corruption to cross borders" (IMF, 2019).

Implementing these strategies through a dharmic lens could involve:

1. Ethical Leadership: Promoting leaders who embody dharmic values of integrity, selflessness, and commitment to the public good.

2. Transparency Initiatives: Implementing comprehensive transparency measures in budgeting, procurement, and public expenditure processes.

3. Citizen Engagement: Encouraging active citizen participation in monitoring public finances and holding officials accountable.

4. Ethical Training: Providing comprehensive ethics training for public officials, emphasizing dharmic principles of integrity and public service.

5. Whistleblower Protection: Implementing robust protections for individuals who report corruption or fiscal mismanagement.

The World Bank suggests additional strategies for combating corruption, including:

1. "Power of the people: Create pathways that give citizens

relevant tools to engage and participate in their governments – identify priorities, problems and find solutions" (World Bank Blogs, n.d.).

2. "Cut the red tape: Bring together formal and informal processes (this means working with the government as well as non-governmental groups) to change behavior and monitor progress" (World Bank Blogs, n.d.).

3. "Get incentives right: Align anti-corruption measures with market, behavioral, and social forces" (World Bank Blogs, n.d.).

Promoting fiscal responsibility involves not only combating corruption but also ensuring that public resources are used efficiently and effectively. This can be achieved through:

1. Robust Budgeting Processes: Implementing comprehensive, transparent budgeting procedures that align with national development priorities.

2. Performance-Based Budgeting: Linking budget allocations to measurable outcomes and performance indicators.

3. Fiscal Rules: Establishing clear fiscal rules and targets to ensure long-term fiscal sustainability.

4. Independent Oversight: Strengthening the role of independent audit institutions and parliamentary oversight committees.

5. Capacity Building: Investing in the skills and capabilities of public financial management professionals.

References

1. Affluent CPA. (n.d.). Principles Of A Good Tax System | Benefits Of Taxation. Retrieved from https://www.affluentcpa.com/principles-good-tax-system/
2. Development Monitoring and Evaluation Office (DMEO). (2022). Accountability and Transparency in Governance.

Retrieved from https://dmeo.gov.in/sites/default/files/2022-04/Thematic_Report_Accountability_and_Transparency_22042022.pdf
3. IMF eLibrary. (n.d.). Tax Policy and Inclusive Growth. Retrieved from https://www.elibrary.imf.org/view/journals/001/2020/271/article-A001-en.xml
4. International Monetary Fund (IMF). (2019). Tackling Corruption in Government. Retrieved from https://www.imf.org/en/Blogs/Articles/2019/04/04/blog-fm-ch2-tackling-corruption-in-government
5. World Bank Blogs. (n.d.). Here are 10 ways to fight corruption. Retrieved from https://blogs.worldbank.org/en/governance/here-are-10-ways-fight-corruption

Chapter 25: Legal Frameworks for the Dharmic Economy

The integration of dharmic principles into legal frameworks offers a promising approach for creating more ethical, sustainable, and socially responsible economic systems. This chapter explores how dharmic concepts can inform corporate law, examines approaches to intellectual property rights that balance innovation with the common good, and discusses dharmic mediation as an alternative dispute resolution mechanism.

Incorporating Dharmic Principles in Corporate Law

Corporate law plays a crucial role in shaping business behavior and economic outcomes. Incorporating dharmic principles into corporate legal frameworks can help create a more ethical and sustainable business environment. Several key dharmic concepts are particularly relevant to corporate law:

1. Dharma (righteousness/duty): The concept of dharma emphasizes fulfilling one's duties and responsibilities in an ethical manner. In corporate law, this principle can be applied to define the duties of directors, officers, and corporations themselves towards various stakeholders.

2. Ahimsa (non-violence): While typically associated with physical non-violence, ahimsa can be extended to corporate conduct, encouraging business practices that avoid harm to stakeholders, communities, and the environment.

3. Aparigraha (non-possessiveness): This principle can inform approaches to corporate ownership and wealth distribution, encouraging more equitable and sustainable business models.

4. Satya (truthfulness): Applied to corporate law, satya supports

transparency, honest reporting, and ethical communication practices.

Implementing these principles in corporate law could involve:

1. Stakeholder-oriented governance models: Expanding directors' duties to consider the interests of employees, communities, and the environment, not just shareholders. This aligns with the dharmic emphasis on interconnectedness and collective well-being.

2. Enhanced corporate social responsibility (CSR) requirements: Mandating more robust CSR initiatives that go beyond philanthropy to address core business impacts. As noted by Agrawal and Kaushik (2023), "Dharma guides organisations to give back to societies by engaging in philanthropic activities as part of CSR initiatives and contributing to social welfare projects and initiatives."

3. Environmental stewardship provisions: Incorporating stronger environmental protection requirements into corporate charters and reporting obligations. This reflects the dharmic principle of ahimsa extended to the natural world.

4. Ethical leadership standards: Developing more comprehensive ethical standards for corporate leaders, drawing on dharmic concepts of righteous conduct.

5. Long-term value creation focus: Encouraging corporate strategies that prioritize long-term, sustainable value creation over short-term profit maximization. This aligns with the dharmic emphasis on considering the long-term consequences of actions.

The integration of dharmic principles into corporate law faces several challenges, including potential conflicts with existing legal frameworks and resistance from those benefiting from the current system. However, as Das argues, "if the state enables the market, the market will reshape society, and the weak state will become strong, in the sense of being compelled by public aspiration to push back on the illiberal aspects of the social order" (Sharma, n.d.). This suggests that incorporating dharmic principles into corporate law could have transformative effects on both business practices and broader societal norms.

Intellectual Property Rights and the Commons

Knowledge as a common resource and intellectual property rights (IPR) are at odds with one another, creating a difficult dilemma for the dharmic economy. Comparatively, dharmic traditions have long stressed the need of free knowledge exchange, in contrast to intellectual property rights (IPR), which seek to encourage innovation by giving temporary monopolies.

The ancient Indian view on the dissemination of information:
As per studies, "Indian scriptures appear to suggest that people of the Indian sub-continent did not uphold the concept of ownership of knowledge and believed that knowledge was to be passed down without reservations: following the parampara (tradition) of the Guru (the erudite teacher) and Sishya (disciple)" (Space and Culture, published in 2000). Knowledge, according to this point of view, should not be seen as a tool for personal gain but as a path to greater spiritual and social progress.

Humans should assist one another in life and prevent each other from making mistakes by sharing their knowledge, according to the Rig Veda. They should do this in the same way that they would share food to prevent starvation (Space and Culture, n.d.). This view casts doubt on the privatization of intellectual property in the contemporary era.

Balancing innovation and the commons:
While the ancient Indian view emphasizes free knowledge sharing, modern economies rely on IPR to incentivize innovation and creativity. A dharmic approach to IPR could seek to balance these competing interests by:

1. Promoting open innovation models: Encouraging collaborative research and development initiatives that share knowledge more freely while still providing incentives for innovation.

2. Expanding fair use and compulsory licensing: Broadening exceptions to IPR for educational, research, and public interest purposes.

3. Shorter protection periods: Reducing the duration of patent and copyright protections to allow knowledge to enter the public domain more quickly.

4. Alternative incentive structures: Developing new ways to reward innovation that don't rely solely on exclusive rights, such as prizes, grants, or tax incentives.

5. Traditional knowledge protections: Developing sui generis systems to protect traditional knowledge and cultural expressions that may not fit within conventional IPR frameworks.

The Creative Commons (CC) movement offers a model for balancing IPR with knowledge sharing. As noted in the research, "The major aim of CC is to allow any person around the globe to access works of knowledge" (Space and Culture, n.d.). This approach allows creators to retain some rights while enabling broader access and use of their works.

Implementing a more dharmic approach to IPR would require significant changes to existing legal frameworks and international agreements. However, as global challenges like climate change and public health crises demonstrate the need for collaborative innovation, there is growing recognition of the limitations of traditional IPR systems.

Dispute Resolution through Dharmic Mediation

Dharmic traditions offer valuable insights for alternative

dispute resolution mechanisms, particularly in the realm of mediation. The concept of dharmic mediation draws on ancient Indian practices of conflict resolution while incorporating modern mediation techniques.

Historical context: Mediation has deep roots in Indian culture, as noted by Ahuja: "The practice of resolving or deciding disputes through mediation or Panchayats was so prominent in the rural parts of the country that both the disputants and the public had full faith in the process" (Ahuja, n.d.). This tradition of community-based dispute resolution aligns closely with dharmic principles of harmony, interconnectedness, and collective well-being.

Key principles of dharmic mediation:

1. Holistic approach: Considering the broader context and relationships involved in a dispute, not just the immediate legal issues.

2. Focus on harmony: Prioritizing the restoration of social harmony and relationships over strict determinations of right and wrong.

3. Ethical conduct: Emphasizing the importance of ethical behavior and fulfillment of duties by all parties involved.

4. Long-term perspective: Encouraging solutions that address underlying issues and promote sustainable resolutions.

5. Interconnectedness: Recognizing the ripple effects of conflicts and resolutions on broader communities and stakeholders.

Implementing dharmic mediation in modern contexts could involve:

1. Training mediators in dharmic principles and their application to dispute resolution.

2. Developing mediation protocols that incorporate dharmic

concepts of duty, harmony, and ethical conduct.

3. Encouraging the use of community elders or respected figures as mediators, drawing on traditional panchayat models.

4. Integrating restorative justice practices that align with dharmic emphasis on healing and reconciliation.

5. Promoting the use of dharmic mediation in various contexts, including commercial disputes, family conflicts, and community disagreements.

Case studies of dharmic mediation: While not explicitly labeled as "dharmic mediation," several examples from Indian history illustrate the potential of this approach:

1. Lord Krishna's mediation: As described by Ahuja, "Lord Krishna, the Supreme God head had himself mediated between the Kauravas and Panda vas to avert the Kurukshetra war" (Ahuja, n.d.). While this mediation ultimately failed, it demonstrates the importance placed on peaceful conflict resolution in Indian tradition.

2. Hanuman's role: In the Ramayana, Hanuman's attempts to mediate between Lord Rama and Ravana offer insights into the challenges and potential of mediation in high-stakes conflicts (MediateGuru, n.d.).

3. Panchayat system: The traditional panchayat system of village-level dispute resolution embodies many principles of dharmic mediation, focusing on community harmony and ethical conduct.

Challenges and considerations: Implementing dharmic mediation in modern legal systems faces several challenges:

1. Balancing traditional practices with modern legal requirements and standards of due process.
2. Addressing power imbalances and ensuring fairness in community-based mediation processes.

3. Adapting dharmic principles to diverse cultural contexts in a globalized world.
4. Integrating dharmic mediation with existing alternative dispute resolution mechanisms and court systems.

Despite these challenges, dharmic mediation offers a promising approach for resolving conflicts in a manner that promotes ethical conduct, social harmony, and long-term well-being.

References:
1. https://www.news18.com/opinion/opinion-the-indianisation-of-corporate-culture-on-the-principles-of-dharma-8671040.html
2. https://caravanmagazine.in/reviews-essays/free-market-dharma
3. https://www.spaceandculture.in/index.php/spaceandculture/article/download/147/pdf_28
4. https://ghconline.gov.in/library/document/conference2728072018/II3IN%20SEARCH%20OF%20TRUE%20'ALTERNATIVE'%20TO%20EXISTING%20.PDF
5. https://nluassam.ac.in/docs/pub/Krishna-and-mediation.pdf
6. https://www.mediateguru.com/post/mission-possible-mediating-the-monumental-battle-in-ramayana
7. https://adikkachannels.com/integrating-sanatana-dharmas-timeless-ethical-principles-with-modern-decision-making/
8. https://main.sci.gov.in/pdf/mediation/MT%20MANUAL%20OF%20INDIA.pdf

Chapter 26: Technology and Innovation in the Dharmic Economy

The rapid advancement of technology and innovation presents both opportunities and challenges for creating a more ethical and sustainable economy. This chapter explores how dharmic principles can inform technological development, guide innovation towards social good, and promote open knowledge sharing.

Ethical Considerations in Technological Development

As technology becomes increasingly powerful and pervasive, ensuring its ethical development and deployment is crucial. Dharmic principles offer valuable insights for addressing the ethical challenges posed by emerging technologies.

Key dharmic concepts relevant to technological ethics include:

1. Ahimsa (non-violence): Extending the principle of non-harm to technological impacts on individuals, society, and the environment.
2. Satya (truthfulness): Promoting transparency and honesty in the development and communication of technological capabilities and risks.
3. Aparigraha (non-possessiveness): Encouraging responsible use of technology and data, avoiding exploitation or excessive accumulation.
4. Karma (action and consequences): Considering the long-term and systemic effects of technological innovations.

Applying these principles to technological development involves several key considerations:

Bias and Fairness: One of the primary ethical challenges in

AI development is addressing bias and ensuring fairness. As noted by Merit Data & Technology (n.d.), AI algorithms can perpetuate and amplify societal biases if not carefully designed and monitored. Ethical AI development must involve:
- Auditing training data for biases
- Monitoring model performance across different demographic groups
- Implementing fairness-aware algorithms during model training
- Regularly assessing AI systems for discriminatory outcomes

Transparency and Explainability: The dharmic principle of satya (truthfulness) emphasizes the importance of transparency in technological development. This is particularly crucial for complex AI systems that may operate as "black boxes." Ethical development requires prioritizing transparency and explainability by:
- Choosing interpretable models when possible
- Providing clear explanations for model predictions
- Documenting model behavior and limitations
- Developing techniques to make complex AI systems more understandable to users and stakeholders

Privacy Protection: The principle of aparigraha (non-possessiveness) can inform approaches to data privacy and protection. Ethical technological development must prioritize robust privacy measures, including:
- Implementing privacy-enhancing techniques such as differential privacy and federated learning
- Minimizing data collection and retention
- Ensuring informed consent for data usage
- Complying with data protection regulations and best practices

Long-term Impact Assessment: The dharmic concept of karma emphasizes the importance of considering the long-term

consequences of our actions. In technological development, this translates to:
- Conducting comprehensive impact assessments that consider social, environmental, and ethical implications
- Implementing ongoing monitoring and evaluation of technological deployments
- Developing frameworks for responsible innovation that prioritize long-term societal benefits

Human-Centered Design: Dharmic principles emphasize the interconnectedness of all beings and the importance of human dignity. Applying this to technological development involves:
- Prioritizing user needs, preferences, and well-being in the design of technological systems
- Ensuring that technology serves human interests rather than the other way around
- Considering the impact of technological innovations on employment and social structures

Environmental Stewardship: The dharmic emphasis on harmony with nature can inform approaches to sustainable technological development. This includes:
- Prioritizing energy-efficient technologies and sustainable manufacturing processes
- Developing technologies that support environmental conservation and regeneration
- Considering the full lifecycle impact of technological products, including disposal and recycling

By integrating these ethical considerations into the technological development process, we can work towards creating innovations that not only advance human capabilities but also promote social good and environmental sustainability.

Innovation for Social Good

The dharmic emphasis on collective well-being and social

responsibility aligns closely with the concept of innovation for social good. This approach seeks to harness technological advancements to address pressing societal challenges and improve quality of life for all.

Key aspects of innovation for social good include:

1. Addressing Unmet Needs: Focusing innovation efforts on solving problems faced by underserved communities or neglected areas of social development.

2. Inclusive Design: Ensuring that technological innovations are accessible and beneficial to diverse populations, including marginalized groups.

3. Sustainable Solutions: Developing innovations that promote environmental sustainability and long-term social resilience.

4. Ethical Business Models: Creating business approaches that prioritize social impact alongside financial sustainability.

Examples of innovation for social good in action include:

1. Telemedicine Platforms: Leveraging digital technologies to provide healthcare access to remote or underserved areas.

2. Clean Energy Solutions: Developing affordable renewable energy technologies for off-grid communities.

3. Assistive Technologies: Creating innovations that enhance the independence and quality of life for individuals with disabilities.

4. Educational Technologies: Developing platforms and tools to improve access to quality education, particularly in resource-constrained settings.

5. Financial Inclusion Technologies: Creating digital banking and financial services solutions for unbanked populations.

The dharmic principle of karma yoga (selfless action) can serve as a guiding philosophy for innovation for social good. This approach emphasizes the importance of working for the benefit of others without attachment to personal gain. Applied to technological innovation, this principle encourages developers and entrepreneurs to prioritize societal impact over pure profit motives.

To promote innovation for social good, several strategies can be employed:

1. Social Impact Incubators: Establishing programs that provide support, mentorship, and resources for startups focused on social innovation.

2. Cross-Sector Partnerships: Fostering collaborations between technology companies, non-profits, and government agencies to address complex social challenges.

3. Impact Investing: Directing capital towards ventures that demonstrate both financial viability and positive social impact.

4. Ethical Innovation Frameworks: Developing guidelines and assessment tools to ensure that technological innovations align with social good objectives.

5. Education and Awareness: Incorporating social impact considerations into technology and entrepreneurship education programs.

By aligning technological innovation with dharmic principles of social responsibility and collective well-being, we can harness the power of technology to create a more equitable and sustainable world.

Open-Source Movements and Knowledge Sharing

The concept of open-source and free knowledge sharing aligns closely with dharmic principles of non-possessiveness (aparigraha) and the belief that knowledge should be freely accessible for the benefit of all. This approach challenges traditional notions of intellectual property and promotes collaborative innovation.

Historical Context: The idea of free knowledge sharing has deep roots in Indian philosophical traditions. As noted in research on intellectual property rights from an ancient Indian perspective:

"Indian scriptures appear to suggest that people of the Indian sub-continent did not uphold the concept of ownership of knowledge and believed that knowledge was to be passed down without reservations: following the parampara (tradition) of the Guru (the erudite teacher) and Sishya (disciple)" (Space and Culture, n.d.).

This perspective aligns with the dharmic emphasis on knowledge as a means of spiritual and societal advancement rather than a source of individual profit.

Modern Open-Source Movements: The open-source software movement, which began in the late 20th century, embodies many of these dharmic principles in a contemporary context. Key aspects of open-source philosophy include:

1. Transparency: Making source code freely available for inspection, modification, and redistribution.

2. Collaboration: Encouraging community-driven development and improvement of software.

3. Non-discrimination: Ensuring that open-source licenses do not restrict who can use, modify, or distribute the software.

4. Integrity: Maintaining the original author's source code while allowing for modifications and derived works.

These principles align closely with dharmic concepts of transparency (satya), collective effort (karma yoga), and non-possessiveness (aparigraha).

Benefits of Open-Source and Knowledge Sharing:

1. Accelerated Innovation: By allowing free access to knowledge and technology, open-source approaches can speed up the pace of innovation and problem-solving.

2. Improved Quality: Collaborative development and peer review can lead to more robust and secure technologies.

3. Increased Accessibility: Open-source solutions can make technology more accessible to individuals and organizations with limited resources.

4. Educational Value: Open access to source code and development processes provides valuable learning opportunities for aspiring technologists.

5. Ethical Alignment: The principles of open-source align with dharmic values of generosity, transparency, and collective benefit.

Challenges and Considerations:

While open-source and free knowledge sharing offer numerous benefits, they also present challenges:

1. Sustainability: Developing sustainable business models around open-source technologies can be challenging.

2. Quality Control: Ensuring the quality and security of open-source projects requires effective governance and community management.

3. Intellectual Property Concerns: Balancing open sharing with the need to protect certain innovations or trade secrets can be complex.

4. Equitable Contribution: Ensuring fair recognition and compensation for contributors to open-source projects is an ongoing challenge.

Promoting Open-Source and Knowledge Sharing: To foster a

culture of open innovation and knowledge sharing aligned with dharmic principles, several strategies can be employed:

1. Educational Initiatives: Incorporating open-source principles and practices into technology education curricula.

2. Corporate Engagement: Encouraging businesses to contribute to and utilize open-source technologies as part of their corporate social responsibility efforts.

3. Government Support: Developing policies that promote the use and development of open-source technologies in public sector projects.

4. Community Building: Fostering vibrant open-source communities through events, hackathons, and collaborative platforms.

5. Ethical Frameworks: Developing guidelines for ethical participation in open-source projects that align with dharmic principles.

By embracing open-source philosophies and knowledge sharing practices, we can create a more collaborative, innovative, and ethically aligned technological ecosystem.

References:
1. Foundations_for_Social_Entrepreneurship_An_Integrative_Indian_Perspective.pdf
2. https://www.spaceandculture.in/index.php/spaceandculture/article/download/147/pdf_28
3. https://spmiasacademy.com/mains_exam/q-4-in-the-quest-of-scientific-and-technological-development-ethical-values-should-not-be-neglected-discuss-it-in-the-current-context-1/
4. https://www.news18.com/opinion/opinion-the-indianisation-of-corporate-culture-on-the-principles-of-dharma-8671040.html

5. https://www.opensourcedharma.info/view/internet-of-dharma
6. https://www.weforum.org/stories/2024/05/successfully-orchestrate-collective-action/
7. https://adikkachannels.com/integrating-sanatana-dharmas-timeless-ethical-principles-with-modern-decision-making/
8. https://adikkachannels.com/ahimsa-paramo-dharma-navigating-the-sacred-balance-of-non-violence-and-duty-in-sanatana-dharma/

Chapter 27: Urban Planning and Sustainable Communities

Urban planning and the development of sustainable communities have become critical issues in the face of rapid urbanization and environmental challenges. This chapter explores how dharmic principles can inform urban design, examines the concept of eco-villages and intentional communities, and discusses approaches to balancing urban development with environmental preservation.

Designing Cities Based on Dharmic Principles

Ancient Indian texts and traditions offer valuable insights for sustainable urban planning that align with dharmic principles of harmony, balance, and interconnectedness. The Mansara Shilpashastra, an ancient treatise on architecture and town planning, provides detailed guidelines for creating well-designed and sustainable urban settlements (Dharma Today, 2017).

Key principles from ancient Indian urban planning that align with dharmic concepts include:

1. Alignment with natural forces: The Mansara emphasizes aligning streets and buildings to maximize the benefits of natural elements like sunlight and wind. For example, main streets were typically oriented east-west to allow purification by the sun's rays (Dharma Today, 2017).

2. Holistic site selection: The Mansara recommends examining potential settlement sites based on multiple factors, including smell, color, shape, direction, sound, and touch. This holistic approach reflects the dharmic understanding of interconnectedness between humans and their environment (Dharma Today, 2017).

3. Social equity and inclusivity: Ancient Indian urban plans often incorporated designated areas for different social groups, reflecting the dharmic principle of fulfilling one's duties based on social position. However, modern interpretations should focus on creating inclusive spaces that promote social equity and community integration.

4. Green spaces and water management: The inclusion of parks, gardens, and water bodies in urban plans aligns with dharmic principles of environmental stewardship and harmony with nature.

5. Sustainable infrastructure: Ancient Indian cities often featured advanced systems for water management, waste disposal, and energy efficiency, reflecting dharmic concepts of responsible resource use.

Implementing these principles in modern urban planning could involve:

1. Biophilic design: Incorporating natural elements and green spaces throughout urban areas to promote well-being and connection with nature.

2. Mixed-use development: Creating diverse neighborhoods that integrate residential, commercial, and recreational spaces, fostering community cohesion and reducing transportation needs.

3. Sustainable transportation: Prioritizing pedestrian-friendly design, cycling infrastructure, and efficient public transit systems to reduce reliance on private vehicles.

4. Energy-efficient buildings: Implementing passive solar design, natural ventilation, and renewable energy systems in urban structures.

5. Water-sensitive urban design: Integrating natural water cycles into urban planning through features like rainwater

harvesting, permeable surfaces, and constructed wetlands.

The city of Chandigarh, designed by Le Corbusier in the 1950s, incorporates some of these principles, blending modern urban planning with traditional Indian concepts. The city's layout features a hierarchical road system, abundant green spaces, and a focus on community-oriented sectors (Dharma Today, 2017).

Eco-villages and Intentional Communities

Eco-villages and intentional communities represent a grassroots approach to creating sustainable living environments based on shared values and ecological principles. These communities often embody dharmic concepts of interconnectedness, simplicity, and harmony with nature.

The Global Ecovillage Network defines ecovillages as "intentional, traditional or urban communities that are consciously designed through locally owned participatory processes in all four dimensions of sustainability (social, culture, ecology and economy) to regenerate social and natural environments" (World Economic Forum, 2022).

Several notable examples of ecovillages and intentional communities demonstrate the potential of this approach:

1. The Farm (Tennessee, USA): Founded on principles of nonviolence, vegetarianism, and respect for the planet, The Farm has become one of the oldest ecovillages in the United States. With 200 residents and 20 Farm-run businesses, it emphasizes community-building, sustainable agriculture, and social activism (World Economic Forum, 2022).

2. EcoVillage Ithaca (New York, USA): Located near downtown Ithaca, this community has achieved an ecological footprint 70% lower than the typical American. It features green buildings, organic farms, and a co-housing model that promotes community interaction and resource sharing (World Economic Forum, 2022).

3. Findhorn Ecovillage (Scotland): Known for its low ecological footprint and sustainable architecture, Findhorn incorporates passive solar features, "breathing walls," and renewable energy systems. The community has been used as a model for "20-minute neighborhoods" where all necessities are within walking distance (World Economic Forum, 2022).

4. Eco Truly Park (Peru): This artistic and spiritual community on the Peruvian coast emphasizes healthy living, yoga, and environmental stewardship. Their Agro Awareness project has transformed sandy soil into a productive organic farm, demonstrating the potential for sustainable agriculture in challenging environments (World Economic Forum, 2022).

These communities showcase several key principles that align with dharmic concepts:

1. Holistic sustainability: Integrating social, economic, and environmental considerations in community design and operations.

2. Participatory governance: Emphasizing collective decision-making and shared responsibility.

3. Spiritual and personal growth: Recognizing the importance of inner development alongside external sustainability practices.

4. Regenerative practices: Focusing on restoring and enhancing natural ecosystems rather than merely reducing harm.

5. Education and outreach: Sharing knowledge and experiences to inspire broader societal change.

While eco-villages and intentional communities may not be suitable for everyone, they serve as valuable living laboratories for sustainable practices and community-building approaches that can inform broader urban planning and development strategies.

Balancing Urban Development with Environmental Preservation

As cities continue to grow and expand, finding a balance between urban development and environmental preservation has become a critical challenge. Dharmic principles of interconnectedness and harmony can inform approaches to this complex issue.

Key strategies for balancing urban development with environmental preservation include:

1. Compact city design: Promoting high-density, mixed-use development to reduce urban sprawl and preserve surrounding natural areas. This approach aligns with dharmic concepts of efficient resource use and minimizing harm to the environment.

2. Green infrastructure: Integrating natural systems into urban environments through features like urban forests, green corridors, and constructed wetlands. This reflects the dharmic understanding of the interconnectedness between human settlements and natural ecosystems.

3. Brownfield redevelopment: Prioritizing the revitalization of previously developed or contaminated sites over greenfield development, preserving undisturbed natural areas.

4. Sustainable transportation: Investing in public transit, cycling infrastructure, and pedestrian-friendly design to reduce reliance on private vehicles and associated environmental impacts.

5. Green building standards: Implementing stringent energy efficiency and sustainability requirements for new construction and renovations.

6. Urban agriculture: Promoting food production within city limits through community gardens, rooftop farms, and vertical farming technologies.

7. Ecosystem services valuation: Incorporating the economic value of natural systems into urban planning and decision-making processes.

Singapore provides an inspiring example of balancing urban development with environmental preservation. Despite its high population density and limited land area, the city-state has implemented innovative strategies to create a livable and sustainable urban environment:

1. Efficient public transportation: Singapore's comprehensive public transit system reduces reliance on private vehicles, minimizing air pollution and energy consumption.

2. Green building initiatives: The city has implemented strict green building standards and incentives, promoting energy efficiency and sustainable design.

3. Urban green spaces: Singapore's "City in a Garden" vision has led to the creation of extensive parks and green corridors, including the iconic Gardens by the Bay.

4. Innovative water management: The country has developed advanced water recycling and desalination technologies to ensure water security while reducing environmental impact.

5. Vertical greenery: Singapore has pioneered the integration of plants into building facades and rooftops, enhancing biodiversity and reducing the urban heat island effect (LinkedIn, n.d.).

These strategies demonstrate how urban development can be pursued in a way that respects and enhances natural systems, aligning with dharmic principles of harmony and interconnectedness.

References

1. Dharma Today. (2017, May

24). Climate Change and Ancient Indian Town Planning. https://dharmatoday.com/2017/05/24/climate-change-ancient-indian-town-planning/
2. LinkedIn. (n.d.). Sustainable Urban Development: Balancing Growth and Environmental Protection. https://www.linkedin.com/pulse/sustainable-urban-development-balancing-growth-environmental
3. World Economic Forum. (2022, September 5). 5 of the World's Coolest EcoVillages. https://www.weforum.org/stories/2022/09/5-of-the-world-s-coolest-ecovillages/

Chapter 28: The Dharmic Economy in a Post-Scarcity World

Questions regarding the future of employment, purpose, and human fulfilment are being prompted by the fast development of technology, especially in the areas of automation and artificial intelligence. This is altering the worldwide economic scene. In this chapter, we look at how dharmic principles might guide our responses to issues like UBI and automation, how we can reimagine employment and purpose in a society that has an abundance of resources, and how we can ensure that our post-scarcity selves find fulfilment in ways other than material possessions.

Addressing Automation and Universal Basic Income

On a grand scale, conventional job patterns are about to be upended by the ever-improving capacities of automation and artificial intelligence. A number of well-known corporations have recently announced massive layoffs, which Forbes says highlights the urgent need for effective solutions. Who or what will secure these restricted places, and will there be enough employment chances for everyone, given that many corporate executives expect further layoffs and a large share intend to replace human workers with AI? That was Rubin in the year 2024.

Job security and the possibility of broad economic displacement are major issues that this technological disruption brings to light. In light of these difficulties, the idea of UBI has been gaining support as a possible remedy. A universal basic income (UBI) would be the systematic and guaranteed provision of a minimum level of living to all residents of a country.

From a dharmic perspective, UBI aligns with several key

principles:

1. Dharma (duty/righteousness): UBI can be seen as fulfilling society's duty to ensure the basic well-being of all its members.

2. Ahimsa (non-violence): By providing a financial safety net, UBI can help mitigate the economic violence of poverty and extreme inequality.

3. Aparigraha (non-possessiveness): UBI encourages a shift away from excessive materialism by ensuring basic needs are met for all.

4. Karma yoga (selfless action): UBI allows individuals to pursue meaningful work and contribute to society without being solely driven by financial necessity.

Implementing UBI in alignment with dharmic principles could involve:

1. Gradual implementation: Introducing UBI through phased approaches, similar to the Alaskan model, to allow for smooth transitions and societal adaptation.

2. Sustainable funding: Developing funding mechanisms that align with dharmic values, such as eco-fiscal policies or targeted taxes on automation-driven profits.

3. Holistic support: Complementing UBI with comprehensive social services and educational programs to support overall well-being and personal development.

4. Ethical considerations: Ensuring that UBI implementation respects individual autonomy and does not create unintended negative consequences.

As noted by experts, UBI has the potential to address several pressing issues in the age of automation:

1. Economic stability: UBI can provide a safety net against economic inequality and insecurity, allowing individuals to

adapt to changing job markets.

2. Mental health: By reducing financial stress, UBI can help mitigate anxiety and other mental health challenges, particularly among young people facing an uncertain job landscape.

3. Innovation and entrepreneurship: With basic needs secured, individuals may be more willing to take risks and pursue innovative ideas or start businesses.

4. Education and skill development: UBI can support lifelong learning and skill acquisition, helping workers adapt to new industries and technologies.

However, implementing UBI also faces challenges, including concerns about affordability, potential impacts on work incentives, and the need to shift societal perceptions about the nature of work and value creation. Addressing these challenges will require careful policy design and ongoing evaluation of UBI pilot programs.

Redefining Work and Purpose in an Abundant Society

As we move towards a post-scarcity world, traditional notions of work and purpose will need to be redefined. The dharmic perspective offers valuable insights for navigating this transition, emphasizing the importance of aligning one's actions with one's true nature and societal well-being.

The concept of swadharma, or one's own duty, provides a framework for understanding work and purpose beyond mere economic necessity. As explained in Swarajya magazine, "Swadharma is that action which is in accordance with your nature. It is acting in accordance with your skills and talents, your own nature (swabhava), and that which you are responsible for (karma)" (Swarajya, n.d.).

In a post-scarcity society, where basic needs are met through

UBI and advanced automation, individuals will have greater freedom to pursue work aligned with their swadharma. This shift could lead to several positive outcomes:

1. Increased innovation and creativity: With financial pressures reduced, people may be more willing to take risks and explore new ideas.

2. Enhanced social contribution: Individuals may be more inclined to engage in volunteer work, community service, or other activities that benefit society.

3. Personal growth and self-realization: Greater freedom to pursue one's true calling can lead to increased personal fulfillment and spiritual growth.

4. Improved mental health: Aligning work with personal values and interests can reduce stress and increase overall well-being.

However, redefining work and purpose in an abundant society also presents challenges:

1. Loss of traditional identity: Many people derive a significant portion of their identity from their jobs, and the transition to a post-scarcity world may require developing new sources of meaning and self-worth.

2. Adapting education systems: Educational institutions will need to shift focus from preparing students for specific careers to fostering adaptability, creativity, and personal development.

3. Addressing inequality: Even in a post-scarcity world, there may be disparities in access to opportunities for meaningful work and personal growth.

To address these challenges, a dharmic approach to redefining work and purpose could involve:

1. Promoting holistic education: Developing educational models that emphasize self-discovery, ethical development, and

adaptable skills alongside traditional academic subjects.

2. Encouraging social entrepreneurship: Supporting initiatives that combine business principles with social impact, allowing individuals to create value for society while pursuing personal fulfillment.

3. Valuing non-traditional work: Recognizing and appreciating contributions to society that may not fit traditional employment models, such as caregiving, artistic pursuits, or community organizing.

4. Fostering community connections: Creating spaces and opportunities for individuals to connect, collaborate, and find shared purpose beyond traditional work environments.

Cultivating Non-Material Sources of Fulfillment

In a post-scarcity world where material needs are largely met, cultivating non-material sources of fulfillment becomes increasingly important. Dharmic traditions offer rich insights into the pursuit of happiness and meaning beyond material acquisition.

The concept of the four purusharthas, or life goals, provides a holistic framework for understanding fulfillment:

1. Dharma (righteousness/duty)
2. Artha (prosperity/wealth)
3. Kama (pleasure/desire)
4. Moksha (liberation/spiritual freedom)

In a post-scarcity society, the focus may shift more towards dharma and moksha, emphasizing ethical living and spiritual growth. As noted in research on dharma, "When life is simple, following dharma becomes simple. When life becomes complex through the influence of ill virtues that we just mentioned above, following dharma becomes very difficult" (EducationPost, 2023). This suggests that a post-scarcity world may actually facilitate the pursuit of dharma by simplifying certain aspects of life.

Strategies for cultivating non-material sources of fulfillment in a dharmic post-scarcity economy could include:

1. Promoting mindfulness and meditation practices: Encouraging widespread adoption of contemplative practices to foster inner peace and self-awareness.

2. Supporting artistic and creative pursuits: Providing resources and opportunities for individuals to explore creative expression as a source of meaning and fulfillment.

3. Emphasizing relationships and community: Creating social structures that prioritize deep human connections and community engagement.

4. Encouraging philosophical and spiritual exploration: Supporting diverse paths of inquiry into life's deeper questions and meaning.

5. Valuing personal growth and self-improvement: Promoting lifelong learning and personal development as core societal values.

6. Fostering environmental stewardship: Encouraging a deep connection with nature and a sense of responsibility for environmental preservation.

As noted by Mark Dawes, "Material success alone may not bring true fulfillment. ... Many spiritual practices focus on cultivating inner peace, mindfulness, and well-being" (Dawes, n.d.). This underscores the importance of balancing material abundance with spiritual and personal development in a post-scarcity world.

The transition to a post-scarcity world presents both immense opportunities and profound challenges for redefining our economic systems and sources of meaning and fulfillment.

By integrating dharmic principles with modern approaches to universal basic income, work redefinition, and non-material fulfillment, we can create a more equitable, purposeful, and spiritually rich society.

As we navigate this transition, it will be crucial to remain flexible, compassionate, and open to new ways of understanding value, work, and human potential. The dharmic emphasis on interconnectedness, ethical living, and spiritual growth provides a valuable framework for creating a post-scarcity world that nurtures both material and non-material well-being for all.

References

1. Dawes, M. (n.d.). The Balance Between Material Success, Happiness and Spiritual Development. LinkedIn. https://www.linkedin.com/pulse/balance-between-material-success-happiness-spiritual-mark-dawes-mjtge
2. EducationPost. (2023, February 25). Dharma Is Closely Related to the Concepts of Duty & Human Service. https://educationpost.in/news/opinion/dharma-vs-religion-vedic-scriptures-takshila-foundation-ryan-baidya
3. Pieri, L. (n.d.). A Roadmap to a Post-Scarcity Society. https://lorenzopieri.com/post_scarcity/
4. Rubin, C. (2024, July 17). Can Universal Basic Income Save Us From The Destabilization Of AI And Automation? Forbes. https://www.forbes.com/sites/cathyrubin/2024/07/17/can-universal-basic-income-save-us-from-the-destabilization-of-ai-and-automation/
5. Swarajya. (n.d.). Hindunomics: From State To Wealth To Dharma To Happiness. https://swarajyamag.com/magazine/hindunomics-from-state-to-wealth-to-dharma-to-happiness

Chapter 29: Global Challenges and Dharmic Solutions

The world faces numerous interconnected global challenges that require holistic solutions. This chapter explores how dharmic principles can inform approaches to addressing climate change, resolving conflicts through economic means, and ensuring food and water security for all.

Addressing Climate Change Through Dharmic Principles

Climate change represents one of the most pressing global challenges of our time. Dharmic traditions offer valuable insights for addressing this crisis through their emphasis on interconnectedness, non-violence, and responsible stewardship of the natural world.

Key dharmic principles relevant to climate action include:

1. Ahimsa (non-violence): Extending the principle of non-harm to encompass the natural environment and future generations.

2. Aparigraha (non-possessiveness): Encouraging sustainable consumption patterns and reducing overconsumption of resources.

3. Karma: Recognizing the long-term consequences of our actions on the climate and taking responsibility for them.

4. Dharma (duty/righteousness): Fulfilling our ethical obligations to protect the planet and its ecosystems.

As noted in the Hindu Declaration on Climate Change, "it is a dharmic duty [to ensure that] we have a functioning, abundant, and bountiful planet" (Ethics and International Affairs, n.d.). This perspective emphasizes the ethical imperative for climate action rooted in religious and cultural values.

Implementing dharmic approaches to climate change could involve:

1. Promoting sustainable lifestyles: Encouraging individuals and communities to adopt more environmentally friendly practices in line with dharmic principles of simplicity and non-possessiveness.

2. Renewable energy transition: Supporting the shift to clean energy sources, reflecting the dharmic emphasis on harmony with nature.

3. Reforestation and ecosystem restoration: Implementing large-scale projects to restore natural habitats, aligning with dharmic concepts of environmental stewardship.

4. Sustainable agriculture: Promoting farming practices that work in harmony with natural systems, reflecting dharmic principles of interconnectedness.

5. Climate education: Incorporating dharmic perspectives on environmental ethics into climate change education and awareness programs.

The Bhumi Project, established by the Oxford Centre for Hindu Studies, demonstrates how dharmic principles can be applied to climate action. The project works to make Hindu pilgrimage sites and worshipping practices more environmentally sustainable, recognizing the unique contributions Hindu teachings can make to addressing climate change (Ethics and International Affairs, n.d.).

Resolving Conflicts and Promoting Peace Through Economic Means

Economic factors often play a significant role in fueling conflicts and instability. Dharmic approaches to economics offer insights for promoting peace and resolving conflicts through more equitable and sustainable economic systems.

Key dharmic principles relevant to conflict resolution through economic means include:

1. Sarvodaya (welfare of all): Prioritizing inclusive economic development that benefits all members of society.

2. Trusteeship: Viewing wealth as a trust to be managed for the benefit of the community rather than for personal gain.

3. Swadeshi (self-reliance): Promoting local economic development and reducing dependence on external resources.

4. Samana (equality): Striving for more equitable distribution of economic resources and opportunities.

Implementing these principles in conflict resolution and peacebuilding efforts could involve:
1. Inclusive economic development: Ensuring that economic growth benefits all segments of society, particularly marginalized groups, to reduce social tensions.
2. Cooperative economic models: Promoting worker-owned cooperatives and other forms of shared ownership to foster economic collaboration across dividing lines.
3. Sustainable resource management: Implementing equitable and sustainable approaches to managing natural resources in conflict-prone regions.
4. Microfinance and economic empowerment: Supporting small-scale entrepreneurship and financial inclusion to create economic opportunities in post-conflict settings.
5. Fair trade initiatives: Promoting ethical trade practices that ensure fair compensation for producers and strengthen local economies.

The Grameen Bank model, founded by Muhammad Yunus, exemplifies how economic empowerment can contribute to peace and stability. While not explicitly based on dharmic principles, the bank's approach to microfinance and poverty alleviation aligns with dharmic concepts of economic justice and collective well-being.

Ensuring Food and Water Security for All

Food and water security are fundamental human rights and essential for global stability and well-being. Dharmic traditions offer valuable perspectives on ensuring equitable access to these vital resources.

The World Bank defines food security as existing "when all people, at all times, have physical and economic access to sufficient safe and nutritious food that meets their dietary needs and food preferences for an active and healthy life" (World Bank, n.d.). This holistic definition aligns with dharmic principles of ensuring the well-being of all beings.

Key dharmic concepts relevant to food and water security include:

1. Anna Brahma (food is divine): Recognizing the sacred nature of food and the importance of equitable distribution.

2. Vasudhaiva Kutumbakam (the world is one family): Emphasizing our shared responsibility to ensure food and water security for all.

3. Ahimsa (non-violence): Promoting sustainable and ethical food production practices that minimize harm to animals and ecosystems.

4. Aparigraha (non-possessiveness): Encouraging responsible use and conservation of water resources.

Implementing dharmic approaches to food and water security could involve:

1. Sustainable agriculture: Promoting farming practices that work in harmony with natural systems, such as agroecology and permaculture.

2. Water conservation: Implementing traditional and modern

water harvesting and conservation techniques inspired by dharmic principles.

3. Equitable distribution: Developing fair systems for allocating food and water resources, prioritizing the needs of the most vulnerable.

4. Reducing food waste: Encouraging mindful consumption and efficient food distribution systems to minimize waste.

5. Community-based food systems: Supporting local food production and distribution networks to enhance food security and resilience.

The work of the Dharma Satya Nusantara Group in Indonesia gives an example of how these concepts might be utilised in practice. As part of its community development initiatives, the firm places an emphasis on food security and alternative livelihoods. It values participatory techniques and pays homage to regions that produce food locally (Dharma Satya Nusantara, n.d.).

Climate change, conflict resolution, food and water security, and other global issues can be better understood by applying dharmic concepts. In order to address these urgent problems in a comprehensive and efficient manner, it is necessary to combine contemporary scientific knowledge with these traditional wisdom traditions.

An ethical framework for climate action may be found in the dharmic emphasis on interconnection, nonviolence, and responsible stewardship; strategies for resolving conflicts through economic means can be informed by the ideals of economic fairness and shared prosperity. Similarly, dharmic ideas about the holiness of food and water and the significance of fair distribution provide direction for making sure everyone has access to these necessities.

We may create more sustainable, peaceful, and egalitarian communities by integrating dharmic knowledge with current scientific and policy methods. This is especially hopeful as we face more complicated global concerns. We may seek answers to global problems by drawing on these ageless principles and updating them for the present world. This will ensure that all living things and the earth are taken care of.

References

1. Dharma Satya Nusantara. (n.d.). Food Security & Alternative Livelihoods. Retrieved from https://dsn.co.id/esg/community-engagement-collaboration/community-development-and-socio-economic-empowerment/food-security-alternative-livelihoods/
2. Ethics and International Affairs. (n.d.). Can Religion Teach Us to Protect Our Environment? Analyzing the Case of Hinduism. Retrieved from https://www.ethicsandinternationalaffairs.org/online-exclusives/can-religion-teach-us-to-protect-our-environment-analyzing-the-case-of-hinduism
3. World Bank. (n.d.). What is Food Security? There are Four Dimensions. Retrieved from https://www.worldbank.org/en/topic/agriculture/brief/food-security-update/what-is-food-security

Chapter 30: Personal Transformation for a Dharmic Economy

The transition to a dharmic economy begins with personal transformation and the cultivation of dharmic values in our daily lives. This chapter explores how individuals can embody dharmic principles through conscious lifestyle choices and actions that contribute to collective transformation.

Cultivating Dharmic Values in Daily Life

Dharmic values provide a framework for ethical living that can guide our actions and decisions in all aspects of life. Key dharmic principles relevant to personal transformation include:

1. Dharma (righteousness/duty): Fulfilling one's responsibilities and ethical obligations.
2. Ahimsa (non-violence): Avoiding harm to oneself, others, and the environment.
3. Satya (truthfulness): Being honest in thought, speech, and action.
4. Aparigraha (non-possessiveness): Cultivating detachment from material possessions.
5. Karma yoga (selfless action): Performing work without attachment to results.

Implementing these principles in daily life involves several practices:

Self-reflection and mindfulness: Regular introspection helps align our actions with dharmic values. As noted by Big Shakti, "Finding your life purpose comes from knowing your dharma, your true nature. It is a process of self-development that engages thinking, feeling, knowing, and doing" (Big Shakti, n.d.).

Ethical decision-making: Considering the broader impact of our choices on others and the environment. Swami Tejomayananda suggests three factors for determining dharmic action:
- Guidance from scriptures
- Societal norms of noble conduct
- Personal peace and joy resulting from the choice (Melwani, n.d.)

Cultivating virtues: Actively developing qualities like compassion, forgiveness, and humility. As Melwani states, "Being loving, kind, honest, forgiving, humble and accepting of others are virtues that we all appreciate in others. Living these virtues is dharma" (Melwani, n.d.).

Fulfilling duties: Performing our responsibilities with the right attitude, regardless of personal preferences. This aligns with the concept of swadharma, or one's own duty, as described in the Bhagavad Gita (Swarajya, n.d.).

Spiritual practices: Engaging in meditation, yoga, or other contemplative practices to deepen our connection with our higher nature.

By integrating these practices into our daily routines, we can gradually transform our consciousness and align our lives more closely with dharmic principles.

Conscious Consumption and Lifestyle Choices

Conscious consumption involves making mindful decisions about what we buy, use, and discard, considering the broader impact of our choices on society and the environment. This approach aligns closely with dharmic principles of non-violence, non-possessiveness, and responsible stewardship.

Key aspects of conscious consumption include:
1. Ethical purchasing: Choosing products and services from companies that align with dharmic values, such as fair labor

practices and environmental sustainability.
2. Minimalism: Embracing a simpler lifestyle that focuses on needs rather than wants, reflecting the dharmic principle of aparigraha.
3. Sustainable living: Adopting practices that reduce our environmental footprint, such as energy conservation, waste reduction, and sustainable transportation.
4. Mindful eating: Choosing food options that are healthy, ethically sourced, and environmentally sustainable.
5. Ethical investing: Aligning financial decisions with dharmic values by supporting socially responsible and environmentally sustainable investments.

Implementing conscious consumption in daily life could involve:

- Researching the ethical and environmental impacts of products before purchasing
- Supporting local and small-scale producers
- Reducing single-use plastics and embracing reusable alternatives
- Adopting a plant-based or reduced-meat diet
- Choosing energy-efficient appliances and renewable energy sources
- Participating in sharing economy initiatives to reduce overall consumption

These lifestyle choices not only align with dharmic principles but also contribute to broader societal and environmental well-being. As noted in the Hindu Declaration on Climate Change, "it is a dharmic duty [to ensure that] we have a functioning, abundant, and bountiful planet" (Ethics and International Affairs, n.d.).

Being the Change: Individual Actions for Collective Transformation

The concept of "being the change" emphasizes the power of

individual actions to catalyze broader societal transformation. This idea aligns closely with the dharmic understanding of interconnectedness and the ripple effects of our actions.

Key principles for being the change include:

1. Leading by example: Embodying dharmic values in our daily lives to inspire others.
2. Taking responsibility: Recognizing our role in creating positive change rather than waiting for others to act.
3. Cultivating awareness: Staying informed about social and environmental issues and their solutions.
4. Engaging in community: Participating in local initiatives and fostering connections with like-minded individuals.
5. Continuous learning and growth: Embracing a lifelong journey of personal development and adaptation.

Practical actions for being the change might include:

- Volunteering for social and environmental causes
- Engaging in civic participation and advocacy for dharmic policies
- Sharing knowledge and skills with others to promote sustainable practices
- Supporting and mentoring others in their personal transformation journeys
- Creating or participating in community initiatives that promote dharmic values

When the sum of many people's acts is large enough, it may have a profound effect. In accordance with the principles of One Earth Sangha, "The sangha—and other forms of social support—are essential: The reality of climate disruption is a profound shock to many people and the only way to minimise or prevent fight, flight, freeze responses is to be supported by and work with others so people will not feel alone, can overcome despair, and develop solutions together" (One Earth Sangha, published in 2012).

A dharmic economy and society can only be built upon the bedrock of personal change. A more ethical, ecological, and satisfying society may be ours when we each make aware consumer choices, cultivate dharmic principles in our everyday lives, and take action for collective reform.

Wisdom contained in dharmic traditions offers helpful direction for relating our individual lives to greater social and environmental welfare as we traverse the complexity of contemporary existence. The path to self-actualization isn't always smooth sailing, but it's worth it for the chances it gives to experience deep satisfaction and make a difference in the world.

In order to bring about a societal and economic transition that is more ethical, ecological, and spiritually linked, it is imperative that we keep investigating and using dharmic concepts in our daily lives.

References:
1. https://www.bigshakti.com/how-to-find-your-life-purpose
2. https://www.manishamelwani.com/what-is-dharma-and-how-to-live-it/
3. https://pmc.ncbi.nlm.nih.gov/articles/PMC3705698/
4. https://www.moneycontrol.com/religion/the-rules-of-dharma-what-they-mean-for-modern-life-article-12879853.html/amp
5. https://oneearthsangha.org/articles/16-principles/
6. https://swarajyamag.com/magazine/hindunomics-from-state-to-wealth-to-dharma-to-happiness

www.ingramcontent.com/pod-product-compliance
Lightning Source LLC
Chambersburg PA
CBHW071021240526
45469CB00006BD/2033